A Geographia Guide

Lake District

**Britain's largest
National Park**

D0367065

INCLUDING

    **KENDAL
PENRITH
KESWICK
DERWENTWATER
BORROWDALE
WINDERMERE
AMBLESIDE
GRASMERE
CONISTON
ULLSWATER
ESKDALE
WASDALE
ENNERDALE
BUTTERMERE**

**Geographia Ltd
63 Fleet Street
London, EC4Y 1PE**

Guide to The Lake District
ISBN 0 09 205350 5
© Geographia Ltd.,
63 Fleet Street,
London, EC4Y 1PE

Compiled and published by
Geographia Ltd

Written by
Roland Taylor

Maps by Geographia Ltd

Photographic illustrations
British Tourist Authority

Series Editor: J. T. Wright

Made and printed in
Great Britain by
The Anchor Press Ltd
Tiptree, Essex

Contents

Illustrations

Photographs

Maps

Every reasonable care has been taken to ensure that the information in this Guide is correct at the time of going to press. Nevertheless, the Publishers can accept no responsibility for errors or omissions or for changes in the details quoted.

Section 1   Introduction

THE LAKE DISTRICT lies in the north-west corner of England,
in the county of Cumbria, originally Cumberland, Westmorland and
part of Lancashire.

The boundaries of the Lake District are the Shap fells to the east,
the Lancashire fells and Morecambe Bay to the south, the Irish
Sea and Solway Firth to the west, whilst to the north is the Border
Country and Hadrian's Wall.

The greatest distance from east to west is forty miles, with a
similar mileage from north to south, but within this small area there
is a greater variety of scenery and a greater number of fine views
than can be found anywhere in the world in so small an area.

At one moment you can be in Wasdale, with its awe-inspiring
ruggedness, two hours later, after walking Sty Head Pass, you meet
with a vivid contrast in the quiet beauty of the Derwent Valley.
From the charming scenery around Windermere or Grasmere, it is but
a few miles to the bold rocky grandeur of the Langdales.

For a Lazy Holiday

The small amount of energy needed to reach and climb the many
points of interest makes the Lake District particularly attractive to
anyone looking for rest and recreation as well as the enjoyment of
the beauties of nature.

For the Energetic

There is plenty of scope for a strenuous holiday, and those who prefer beauty to excitement will find the smallness of the Lake District a great advantage.

A fair knowledge of the District can be gained during a week's walking, you can cycle round it in a day, or motor round it in a few hours. On the other hand, many months can be spent here, with discoveries of fresh beauties every day.

For the Solitary

The Lake District is essentially a place where an open-air holiday in peace and quietness can be enjoyed, far from the rush of city life.

In season large numbers of visitors frequent the more popular places—Bowness-on-Windermere, Ambleside and Keswick, and also some of the lakes—Ullswater, Coniston and Tarn Hows, while on the main roads there is a continuous stream of traffic. In the heart of Lakeland, hemmed in by lofty fells and towering screes, the solitude and quiet of the District can still be found.

Not for the motorist or day-tripper is the call of the raven, the murmur of mountain becks, the bleating of sheep, the scent of heather and bracken or the feel of the springy turf. These joys, so dear to the heart of the true lover of the open spaces, are solely for those who see the Lake District on foot.

Leaving the main road between Keswick and Windermere and travelling west, the solitary places become more and more frequent. Here and there the moors and fells cluster round, as though jealously guarding the lakes and tarns whose only shadows are the reflections of the surrounding hills and whose only ripples are caused by the mountain trout jumping for flies. There are no tarmac roads here, only rough cart tracks leading from one farm to another; and the paths across the fells made by countless numbers of walkers over many years, or the tiny footmarks of the sheep.

For the Non-Walker

For those who do not wish to walk far, the Lake District can still provide plenty of attractions; there are cinemas in Keswick, Ambleside, Windermere and the gateway towns. Dances are held in most of these places, and the visitor will find there a strange contrast in the lively country dances to the staid affairs that are usually found in the towns and cities. Boating can be enjoyed on many of the lakes and there is plenty of outdoor sport.

The Dialect

The visitor from the south and Midlands of England will notice another difference—the dialect. Words unknown in the south of England are used, a mountain or hill is a fell, a rocky hill a crag, brooks and streams are becks, pools and small lakes are tarns. A ravine with a stream in it is called a ghyll. We shall use these words throughout this guide to help the visitor feel the atmosphere of the Lake District even before he gets there.

A glossary of the local names is sold at Information Centres.

HOW TO GET THERE

The usual entry to the Lake District is by Kendal and Windermere from the south and the Midlands, and by Penrith and Keswick from the north.

By Rail

British Rail runs trains to Kendal, Windermere, and Penrith from Euston during the summer, calling at Crewe (where there are connections from Birmingham), Warrington, Wigan, Preston and Lancaster. There are also trains from Liverpool, Manchester and other districts. It may be necessary to change trains at Oxenholme or elsewhere.

There are also through trains from Euston and the above stations to Penrith, which lies on the main L.M.R. line between Euston and Carlisle. It is necessary to go by service bus between Penrith and Keswick or Ullswater.

There are also trains up the West Coast from Preston and other stations, passengers changing into a bus at Ulverston for Lake Side where a launch meets it to sail up the lake to Bowness and Waterhead (Ambleside), summer service only. For Coniston change at Foxfield and proceed by bus; for Eskdale change at Ravenglass, where the Ravenglass and Eskdale miniature railway will convey you through seven miles of picturesque scenery into the heart of Eskdale; this train only runs during the summer months. There is a regular service between Easter and October, but during the winter there is only one train a day in either direction. A timetable may be obtained from the Manager, Ravenglass and Eskdale Railway, Ravenglass, Cumbria.

Local Services

Easy though it is to reach the main towns by rail, transport within the district is not good, excepting on the outskirts; the only line inside the Lake District is between Kendal and Windermere, although there is a short private line between Haverthwaite and Lake Side which operates during the summer months. British Rail operate the modern launches which sail the full length of Windermere daily at frequent intervals in summer. Motor yachts of the Ullswater Navigation and Transit Company ply the full length of Ullswater during the summer months and there are several motor launches sailing round Derwentwater.

By Bus

The Lake District is well served by bus services. The Ribble Motor Services run express coaches from the principal towns in the north to Penrith, Kendal, Keswick, Grasmere, Ambleside and Windermere.

The same company operates a useful daily service of buses in the southern and central parts of the district as far as Keswick; practically every town and village from Keswick to Kendal, Ambleside to Coniston, Langdale and Ulverston, is covered by this service.

The service between Keswick and Penrith is owned jointly with Cumberland Motor Services Ltd., whose buses cover the district from Keswick to West Cumberland, Ullswater, Seatoller, Buttermere and Carlisle. Both services have a joint station at Keswick. Thus, using these services, it is possible to reach almost every lake and valley at little cost and within a very reasonable time. Some run only during the Easter and summer periods and visitors are advised to obtain timetables from the respective head offices, Ribble Motor Services, Ltd., Frenchwood Avenue, Preston, and Cumberland Motor Services, Ltd., Tangier Street, Whitehaven.

There are several minibus services, which are extending and include Windermere to Eskdale and Wasdale, Keswick and Glenridding, via Newlands from Keswick to Buttermere, and others not covered by the major companies. Timetables giving full details are available from Mountain Goat Service, Windermere, who also organise extended holiday sightseeing tours.

It must be borne in mind that these services may vary considerably and it is always advisable to make prior enquiries locally.

WALKING

The Lake District is undoubtedly the walkers' paradise; every year, increasing numbers of people tramp its fells and its dales, people of all ages and from all walks of life, some paying the Lakes a first visit, but many coming back after years of regular holidays there.

Unlike some other districts in Britain, there is no restriction of access, the walker is free to wander over the fells and in the dales as desired; provided he shuts gates after him, does not tramp across cultivated lands, and does no damage, it is unlikely that anyone will interfere with him.

In this book walks are graded into three classes: (a) Easy—walks which can be done in two or three hours by any normal person; (b) Moderate—rather longer walks of six to twelve miles involving little or no climbing; (c) Strenuous—usually includes fell climbing, which could only be undertaken by those used to walking.

Those used to comparatively flat country will find a great change on a first visit to the Lakes, and in planning a walk should remember to take into consideration the gradients. A twelve to fifteen miles tramp on the fells may equal a twenty-five miles tramp over flat country, so until you become used to fell climbing and leg muscles are acclimatized to climbing and dropping it is wise to keep mileage down; twelve to fifteen is quite a good average for a day on the fells.

The walker has two methods of seeing the Lake District. He can either take an extended tour, or he can stay at a centre and go out from there each day.

Guided Walks

Guided walks are organized regularly during the summer season from Waterhead, Ambleside, Bowness, Buttermere, Coniston, Hawkshead, Keswick, Seatoller, Glenridding, White Moss Common (near Grasmere), and other centres. Most of these walks are short and easy, but more strenuous walks often commence at Keswick. Full details of these walks are available from the National Park Information Centres, or by post from The Information Officer, Church Street, Windermere.

Extended Tours

The advantages of making an extended tour is that a greater area of country can be covered; each day is fresh, no previous ground having to be gone over at the beginning of the walk as frequently happens from a centre, and the Youth Hostels make this type of holiday an easy achievement. Disadvantages are that you have to complete your journey whatever the weather may be and that most of your luggage has to be carried on the back; some of this can be eliminated by posting on a change of clothes to one of the points where you intend to spend a night.

By staying at a centre, you only carry with you each day goods that are necessary such as lunch, a waterproof, map, whistle, compass and perhaps a change of socks.

Clothing

In the warmer weather, the ideal clothing for walking is a pair of shorts, a short-sleeve shirt or blouse, and an anorak for warmth. Often, even in summer, the weather can change very quickly and it is advisable to carry extra clothing, such as woollen slacks—the stretch nylon type and cotton jeans are condemned by doctors as being unsuitable, and they can be killers because they do not retain the heat of the body should the wearer be caught out on the fells for any lengthy period, a warm pullover should also be carried. In

cooler weather and in the winter, slacks or knee breeches are the best
wear, and two thin pullovers under an anorak are warmer than one
thick one.

Remember that most anoraks are only shower proof and will not
withstand heavy rain; in wet weather, additional waterproofs,
including overtrousers, should be carried, but only worn in the rain
as they are not porous and therefore can be unhealthy.

Always wear proper walking boots on the fells, improper footwear
is the greatest cause of fell accidents. Two pairs of thick wool socks
are more comfortable than one. Most walking boots are made
sufficiently large to take the two.

Fell Walkers' Code

Study the fell walkers' code. Copies are displayed in many places
throughout the Lake District, or can be obtained from the Lake
District Mountain Accidents Association. It is important that, if you
fail for any reason to return to your destination, you notify someone
before nightfall, the police if no one else is convenient, otherwise a
search team may be called out to look for you.

There are many alternative routes for extended walking tours, and
later in the book there are suggestions for walks from centres which,
if desired, could be incorporated in other walking tours.

Youth Hostels

There is a splendid chain of about 30 Youth Hostels available to
members of the Association. Those using the hostels have to perform
certain light duties each day, and conform to its rules;
accommodation is limited to a maximum of three days at any one
hostel. All types of buildings form these hostels. Some, such as
Eskdale and Longthwaite (Borrowdale), have been built specially
for the purpose, others are converted hotels, mills and shepherds'
huts or simply part of a farm.

Members of the Ramblers Association and affiliated clubs can also
stay at the Gordon Walker Chalet at Stair, Newlands Valley. (Holds 16).

Because Youth Hostels form one of the cheapest and best means
of accomplishing extended tours, the following is planned so that
there is a Youth Hostel at the end of each day's tramp, but those
who prefer extra comfort will find ample accommodation at the farms
and inns in each district.

First Day. Coniston, Tilberthwaite Ghyll, Tom Ghyll, Tarn Hows,
track from north end of the tarn along Oxenfell Road by the new
National Trust footpath to Elterwater. *9 miles.*

Second Day. Little Langdale Tarn, Wrynose Pass, Cockley Beck,
Hard Knott Pass, Eskdale. *8 miles.*

Third Day. Visit Stanley Ghyll. From Boot village, proceed up the right side of Whillan Beck to Ghyll Bank and Buckpot Falls. Over Burnmoor to Wasdale Head, Sty Head Pass, Seathwaite, Seatoller. Longthwaite Hostel. *11 miles (excluding visit to Stanley Ghyll which is a mile each way).*

Fourth Day. Bowder Stone, Grange Fell, Watendlath, Ashness Bridge, via lake shore to Friar's Crag, Keswick. *9 miles.*

Fifth Day. Proceed over Newlands to Buttermere. Climb Wandope, Grasmoor, Sail, Causey Pike, Keswick. *8 miles.*

Sixth Day. Bus to Rosthwaite. Walk Stonethwaite, Greenup Ghyll, Greenup, High White Stones, Harrison Stickle, Easedale Tarn, Grasmere. *9½ miles.*

Seventh Day. Grisedale Tarn, Dollywaggon Pike, Helvellyn, Striding Edge, Patterdale. *8 miles.*

This tour can be extended by staying at one place two nights and doing a fell climb the second day, or it can be shortened by missing out the fifth and seventh day itinerary. All the routes in the tour are well marked, and a one inch to the mile, or a 1: 25,000 Leisure Map of the Lake District (4 sheets) will be found an invaluable help. It is unwise for strangers to go on the fell tops in cloudy weather. A compass is always useful, especially when mist comes down unexpectedly. Always take one with you when you climb.

MOTORING

There is a good motoring road through the Lake District from Kendal by way of Windermere, Ambleside and Grasmere to Keswick. There is another good road that fringes the area, and the road between Windermere and Penrith by Kirkstone Pass is also quite good.

Motorists will find the A66 trunk road offers speedy access from Penrith to Keswick, Cockermouth and the Western Lakes.

Secondary roads with a good surface lead up several of the valleys, many of these are hilly and narrow, but the motorist who is prepared to drive slowly and with care will find it very pleasant, and most parts of the district can be reached by them.

Only a few of the passes should be attempted; main roads go over Dunmail Raise and Kirkstone Pass; on the Grasmere and Ullswater and Ambleside sides respectively the gradient is steep, the other sides moderate. When doing the popular Windermere-Keswick circle, go by Kirkstone to Ullswater, on to Keswick and back to Windermere by Dunmail. Whinlatter Pass is also quite good, there is a sharp gradient on either side, Braithwaite side being the worst. Honister, Newlands, Hard Knott and Wrynose Passes have good surfaces, but are steep and dangerous in parts. Hard Knott has many sharp bends and should be avoided by timid drivers. The steepest part of Honister is on the Buttermere side near the top, and on the Keswick side of Newlands, gradients being about one in three or four. All other passes are unfit and inaccessible to the motor car.

Lakes

Nearly all the larger lakes can be reached by car, in fact, the main roads run along the shores of many and the motorist who is content to view the fells from below will find much to interest him, especially if he is prepared to stop the car frequently and walk around.

The following suggestions for visiting the Lakes quickly may be found useful by the visitor paying his first visit.

Tour 1 : Kendal, Windermere, Ambleside, Grasmere, Keswick, Whinlatter Pass to Buttermere. Return to Scale Hill, Loweswater, Lamplugh, Croasdale, Ennerdale, Cold Fell, Calderbridge, Gosforth, Wastwater (keep left all the way from Gosforth), Strands, Santon Bridge, Eskdale, Birker Moor, Ulpha, Broughton, Coniston, Hawkshead, Ferry, Windermere, Kendal. *121 miles.*

Tour 2 : Kendal, Windermere, Kirkstone Pass, Ullswater, Penrith or Troutbeck, Keswick, Grasmere, Windermere, Kendal. *73 miles.*

Tour 3 : Kendal, Lake Side, Esthwaite Water, Hawkshead, Coniston, Skelwith Bridge, Little Langdale, Elterwater, Red Bank, Grasmere, Windermere, Kendal. *63 miles.*

CYCLING

The wise cyclist will leave the main roads wherever possible, for the narrow winding secondary roads have good surfaces, avoid the heavy motor traffic and are much more pleasant and interesting to ride along.

One thing is essential, however, brakes must be in perfect condition, for many hills are steep with nasty bends at the bottom; a variable gear is also a great asset.

The passes already referred to in the paragraph on motoring also apply to the cyclist. In addition, those who do not object to pushing their machines both up and down will find Hard Knott and Wrynose

Passes possible, the surface is good but the gradients are very steep
in parts. It is also possible to push cycles over Garburn and Walna
Scar passes, but they are not recommended; on all other passes the
only way to take a cycle over is to shoulder the machine and carry it.

Exploration
The cyclist who desires to explore the lakes in a short period may
follow the routes already planned for the motorist, about seventy
miles in a day is sufficient to really enjoy cycling in this district,
frequent halts being necessary to appreciate the beauty and views.

Another tour for the cyclist which avoids many of the main roads
is as follows:

Kendal to Newby Bridge, Lake Side, Esthwaite Water, Hawkshead,
Tarn Hows, Coniston, Colwith Force, Little Langdale Tarn, Blea
Tarn, Dungeon Ghyll, Elterwater, Red Bank, Grasmere, Dunmail
Raise, left side of Thirlmere, Keswick, Borrowdale, Honister Pass,
Buttermere, Scale Hill, Loweswater, Lamplugh, Kirkland, Ennerdale,
Cold Fell, Calderbridge, Gosforth, Wastwater, Santon Bridge,
Eskdale, Ulpha, Wrynose Pass, Ambleside, Kendal. The distance is
about 140 miles, and includes most of the lakes with the exception
of Brotherswater, Ullswater, and Haweswater. The latter can be
included by extending the tour from Ambleside over Kirkstone Pass
to Brotherswater, Ullswater, and Penrith. To visit Haweswater,
there is only one road from Penrith, the return being made along
the same route. From Penrith, the main road over Shap could be
followed to complete the round at Kendal.

HOLIDAY CENTRES
The principal centres are Keswick, Ambleside and Windermere, all
small towns whose main industry is catering for visitors; there are
good transport facilities to and from all these places. Smaller centres
are Grasmere, Buttermere, Ullswater, Eskdale, Coniston and
Borrowdale, but apart from providing accommodation there are no
indoor amusements. On the outskirts are several small towns, Kendal,
Grange-over-Sands, Ulverston, Arnside, Cockermouth and Penrith,
all interesting in themselves. Some of the farms in Ennerdale provide
accommodation, but the nearest town is Whitehaven, ten miles away.

Accommodation
There is ample accommodation to suit every taste, from the
high-class hotel to the lowly farmhouse; bookings at all places are
heavy at Easter, Whitsun and in July and August, and it is advisable
to book well in advance.

View Points

The Lake District is famous for its view points, which fall into two categories. There is the view looking up to the fells from the valleys, and the view from the top of the fells looking down the dales; it would be difficult to say which was the finer. The former is one of magnificent grandeur, many of the fells viewed from the dales leave a lasting impression, and it is for this reason that the majority of Lakeland dales are best approached from the bottom, so that you have the view of the fells ahead all the time.

Some of the best views which come under this class include the Langdale Pikes viewed from near Elterwater, the same Pikes viewed from Blea Tarn and, farther away, from Tarn Hows. Derwentwater and Skiddaw with Bassenthwaite Lake in the background is a popular view from Ashness Bridge or from Gowder Crag, a little higher up.

Another impressive and magnificent view, especially in the clear weather, is from the shores of Wastwater looking towards Wasdale Head with a background formed by such famous fells as Yewbarrow, Great Gable, Great End, Lingmell, Scafell Pikes and Scafell, and the Screes. Others are St. Sunday Crag from the Howtown side of Ullswater, Fleetwith Pike and Haystacks from Buttermere, Grasmere from Red Bank or Silver How and Windermere and Coniston from a point near Tarn Hows.

The fell-top view gives one an impression of space, and it is here one realizes how small and compact the Lake District really is. It is fascinating to identify the various peaks, which have altered greatly in appearance since viewed from below. From many peaks it is possible to see three to five lakes; the Irish Sea, Morecambe Bay and Solway Firth are to be seen from those in the west, also the Scottish and Yorkshire hills, and on very clear days the Isle of Man, Welsh mountains and the Mountains of Mourne in Ireland; the latter can only be seen on very rare, exceptionally clear days from Bowfell, Scafell and other western fells.

GEOLOGY

The Lakeland mountains are the remains of a very old upthrust system, whose main axis lies roughly from west to east, across Scafell and Helvellyn, with a subsidiary summit to the north corresponding with Skiddaw. It is considered that Lakeland is one of the oldest masses in the world. The fells have a more ancient lineage than the Alps, Andes or Himalayas; Skiddaw is considered to be the oldest mountain in Europe and along with Black Combe and the Long Mynd in Shropshire it is among the veteran mountains of the world.

The central district consists mainly of volcanic rocks composed of highly compressed ash with a bluish-green tinge in much of it. On the west are two zones of igneous rock, the Eskdale and the Ennerdale granite, both of which are characterized by their pinkish hue. Across the north and north-west is a belt of slate—Saddleback, Skiddaw, Grasmoor and Black Combe.

Here and there faults in the strata have become filled with drifts of ore, and we get red deposits in Ruddy Ghyll between Grain Ghyll and Esk Hause, in the gully of Lord's Rake on Scafell and Red Pike above Buttermere; much of the Ennerdale fells contains this red ore.

The Ice Age was the last epoch during which the sculpture of these mountains and valleys took place. On many of the fells you will see scratches caused by the glaciers, which, as they receded, left behind those curious conical mounds of drift, old moraine heaps, to be seen at the head of the Liza Valley or in Greenup Ghyll near Borrowdale.

On the sea coast are the remains of what are called submerged forests. These are accumulations of peat and trunks below high water mark, evidently on the site where they grew.

The Borrowdale rocks were distributed by an immense volcano, which operated somewhere in the region of Keswick, but has long since been denuded away; some of its minor vents survive of which Castle Head is probably one, while Walla Crag and Falcon Crag feature as the best of the lava beds. This volcano was probably larger than Etna, which is 10,000 feet high and thirty miles in circumference. Some 15,000 feet of material was erupted from this Lakeland crater, providing the rocks from which has been carved the glorious scenery of Wastwater, Eskdale, Ennerdale, Ullswater, Langdale and Thirlmere areas.

Notice how the ice persisted on the sunless sides of the hills, facing north and east, and these sides are now mainly crags and cliffs which contrast so greatly with the more grassy slopes facing the south and west.

So the story goes on, with rain, frost and snow, and the daily alternations of cold and heat, each still chiselling out the features of the landscape. Rivers carry away the wastage and contribute to the beauty of the lakes by forming deltas of material, many of which are tree-clad, providing picturesque features in the scene.

ARCHAEOLOGY

The Lake District is covered with many prehistoric remains, stone circles, cairns and hut circles, 'the homes of the silent vanished race' There are several fine remains of Neolithic stone circles, a reminder of the days when the people of this country worshipped the sun. One is situated about a mile and a quarter from Keswick in the

direction of Penrith, a second, Swinside, lies near the eastern end
of Black Combe, and a third on the side of the main fell road between
Ennerdale and Calderbridge. North-east of Penrith are the famous
'Long Meg and her Daughters'. Several Roman roads traverse the
district, the most notable being the road from near Windermere
which crosses the range of mountains named High Street in the
direction of Penrith; another, probably a branch of the High Street
road, goes from Ambleside over Wrynose and Hard Knott passes to
Ravenglass. There are traces of several others. Hard Knott Fort,
situated on the side of that pass, is one of the best remaining examples
of the forts built by the Romans.

At Ravenglass stands the remains of an old Roman bath-house,
one of the finest examples of this type of building in the country.
Near the ancient bridle road from Waberthwaite to Ulpha are to
be found the remains and foundations of pre-Roman hut circles and
burial cairns; more lie on the side of Boat How, and Lankrigg in the
Calder and Wormghyll valleys.

High up on Stake Pass, and on Scafell Pike, New Stone Age
axe-makers of nearly 4,000 years ago had axe factories, from which
were exported beautifully made axes to as far afield as Wiltshire,
Dorset and Yorkshire; there was another factory at Portinscales.

SPORT AND RECREATION

The Lake District does not claim to provide elaborate indoor
amusements; there are no super cinemas, theatres or ballrooms,
dances are usually held in the village hall or in the school, but what
the room lacks in splendour is more than compensated for by the
jolly, lively atmosphere of the dance itself.

The great attractions are the outdoor sports, which have big
followings, not football and cricket—excepting in the towns—but
hound trailing, fox-hunting, beagles and otter hunts, and the annual
sports.

Hound Trailing

Hound trailing is a sport which appears to be found only in this
district. The hounds, specially bred for the purpose, follow the
scent of a trail which is laid by a man walking round the course in
the morning dragging a wet sack full of aniseed. The start and finish
of a trail are very thrilling, the dogs line up, straining every muscle,
all keyed up to be off. The course is usually ten to twelve miles long,
and when it is laid round the fell-sides the dogs can be seen most
of the time. During the race the dogs are entirely on their own, but
about half a mile from the finish the owners are allowed to shout and

whistle. There is great excitement when the dogs come into the last lap, and much shouting and whistling as they race to the finish, where they are rewarded with a feed.

These trails are held all over the district during the summer and there is a league championship table.

Foxhunting

Foxhunting takes place during the winter, and the foxhounds, which are beautiful animals, are bred quite differently from the trail hounds. Owing to the nature of the country the dogs must be followed on foot, and provide good exercise for the followers. Many spectators prefer to climb to some good vantage point from where they can follow the course of the hounds without much exertion.

There are five packs of these foxhounds; the Blencathra, Coniston, Eskdale and Ennerdale, Melbreak and the Ullswater.

Sports Days

These annual events are held during the late summer in many of the villages and are wonderful affairs. They usually include a show of livestock and local products, flat racing, wrestling in the Cumberland and Westmorland style, sometimes a sheepdog trial, a fell race, which is one of the most strenuous of all races, the competitors having to race to the summit of one of the fells and back, and it is common for competitors to fall out before the finish. The sports day generally finishes with the hound trail and a dance.

One of the most famous of these sports days is held at Grasmere in August.

Fishing

Fishing is good and can often be obtained in the lakes and rivers. Trout fishing is best enjoyed in the spring, at Ullswater, Buttermere and Loweswater. Nearly all the lakes teem with perch, notably Derwentwater, Bassenthwaite, Windermere, Rydal and Esthwaite. The fell becks sometimes yield fair baskets of small trout to the upstream worm fisher.

For salmon, sea-trout and herling the angler must seek the lower reaches of the Derwent, Irt, Ehen, Duddon and the Lune. The Derwent is the best, but most of it is in private hands. Sea-trout fishing is at its height from the third week in July until the end of August, herling mostly in August and summer salmon from July onwards.

Most of the fishing rights are held by riparian owners or by angling associations, and it is necessary to obtain a licence or become temporary members of the local angling association.

Fuller information about fishing in the Lake District may be obtained from the fishing-tackle dealers in the various centres.

B

BIRDS

Although the Lake District is a comparatively small area, the altitude varies up to 3,000 feet above sea-level, and it includes valleys mountains, swamps, lakes and rivers, so that the bird life varies accordingly. In the vales most of the birds common to Northern England are represented, with a few notable exceptions. The green woodpecker is unknown, but the green-spotted is a familiar figure in the woodlands. The lesser whitethroat, chiffchaff and blackcap are very local, whereas their relatives, the common whitethroat, willow warbler and garden warbler are found throughout the area. The house sparrow is rare in many of the dales, its place being taken by the chaffinch, which may be considered the typical Lakeland bird.

Ring Ouzel

The pied flycatcher is to be found around Ullswater, yellow-hammers are very local and almost unknown in some of the dales whereas in low areas the wheatears and meadow pipits are every-where, and the wild screech of the ring ousel is only heard in areas where heather is abundant. Below 600 feet the tree pipit is common, and above that height the meadow pipit takes its place, seldom do their territories overlap. The latter calls 'thrip-thrip' but if no 'r' is heard it is the tree pipit. Skylarks are common in the wild dales but shun the shut-in areas.

Kestrel

On the high fells the 'kraak' of the ravens and the 'meew' of the buzzards are often heard, the former are common in the Buttermere valley; the peregrine and the merlin still manage to exist, while the kestrel and sparrowhawk abound. Jays and magpies are common in the Windermere district, but are seldom seen around Ullswater; yellow-hammers and house sparrows are also peculiar to selected districts.

Owls

Other typical Lakeland birds are the dippers and wagtails, which can be found by almost any river. In wooded areas are the wood warblers, golden-crested wrens and tree creepers, or tree mouse as they are locally called. Towards evening, owls are often in evidence, a white shadow flitting past on noiseless wings tells of a barn owl on the hunt, while the melodious hoot of the brown owl is a familiar sound. The long-eared owl is also known, but is such a silent and elusive bird that it often escapes notice; the nightjar is confined to certain areas and is rarely heard.

Gullery

At Ravenglass is a famous gullery where various types of seagulls, including the tern, breed in a protected area; permission to visit it may be obtained from the Cumberland County Council, The Courts, Carlisle.

ANIMALS

Among the common animals is the badger, which frequents the woods and delights in uprooting the nests of wild bees for the honey; it is found in all parts of the district.

The Otter

The otter is more rare than the badger, but can sometimes be seen in the river; he shuns observation, and unless he is in a country that is little disturbed he is not given to fishing in daylight. He is a

harmless and singularly fascinating beast. He kills few fish as he cannot outswim a healthy, vigorous salmon or trout, and his only way of taking them is to pounce on them as they ascend a sloping weir apron. He feeds largely on eels and carrion.

The Fox

The fox is another animal common in the district; occasionally the walker will see a fox stealing away from his look-out place on a protruding crag or see him jump up in the heather on one of the terraces of the fells.

NATIONAL PARK

In 1951, 866 square miles of the Lake District became a National Park, the largest in Britain. This means that its fine landscape has been marked out for special planning care aimed at two prime purposes: to preserve and enhance its natural beauty and to promote its enjoyment by the public.

The Lake District Special Planning Board, which administers the National Park, works in many different way to achieve these purposes. They maintain appropriately high planning standards by paying special attention to design and materials, to siting, and to screening and sometimes, when necessary, to safeguard landscape beauty, by refusal of permission. They may make arrangements for the provision of accommodation, meals and refreshments, where existing facilities are considered to be inadequate. They may lay out camping sites and parking places, remove eyesores and so on.

The National Park Rangers and corps of voluntary wardens are also ready and willing to point out the way and to give advice and help to visitors.

England's highest fells, Scafell Pike, Helvellyn and Skiddaw, are in the Lake District National Park. Walking and rock climbing are the principal recreations. But those unfamiliar with the fells and the vagaries of the climate should seek the advice of local folk or of experienced walkers before setting out for a day on the fells.

Important

It is most important for visitors to remember that the normal life of those who live and work in the National Park goes on, and to understand that although the area is a National Park the ownership of land has not changed. Walkers, climbers and picnickers should note that the farmers' fields are, and will remain, as private inside the National Park as elsewhere. You should, wherever possible, keep to the paths, close all gates and observe the Country Code. Remember, too, that one of the attractions of the Lake District is the stillness of the fells—do not play transistor radios out of doors.

Brockhole

In 1969, the first National Park Centre in Britain was opened at Brockhole, a large mansion which is roughly halfway between Ambleside and Windermere on the lake side of the main road. It is easily recognized by the large notice and car park at the entrance. Parking is free but there is a small charge for admission. Open March to October.

The building is a magnificent mansion in spacious grounds over-looking Windermere, with the Langdale Pikes in the distance. There is a boat landing in the grounds.

Inside the building is an ever changing show of the Lake District in

all its aspects. There are diagrams and models, relief maps, drawing
and slide shows all running automatically. Another deals with rock
climbing, the industries of Lakeland, its history covering 4,000 years,
bird life, fish, animals, and views of the district. There is also a stall
for the distribution and sale of literature, books and maps, and
refreshments can be obtained in the café or in the picnic area in
the grounds.

The gardens are among the most immaculate in the north of
England and are themselves worth a visit. The picnic site is complete
with seats and tables. There are 32 acres of grounds to wander
through reaching down to the lake shore.

INFORMATION CENTRES

During the summer, information service caravans and offices,
operated by the Lake District Planning Board, are open at Bowness,
Glenridding, Waterhead, Ambleside, Hawkshead, Seatoller and
Keswick.

The National Trust have information offices at Bridge House,
Ambleside: Derwentwater Boat Landing, and Grasmere.

Others may be opened in the near future.

Further information about these may be obtained from the Lake
District Information Office, Windermere, or the National Trust,
Borrans Road, Ambleside.

ENGLISH TOURIST BOARD

A network of Tourist Information Centres exists throughout
England. Each displays a sign, a red Tudor rose with the words
'Tourist Information' on a blue ground. This is the symbol of the
English Tourist Information Services.

Addresses of these offices are quoted in this Guide. Many centres
maintain a Tourist Accommodation Service—available to personal
callers only. This is indicated thus:

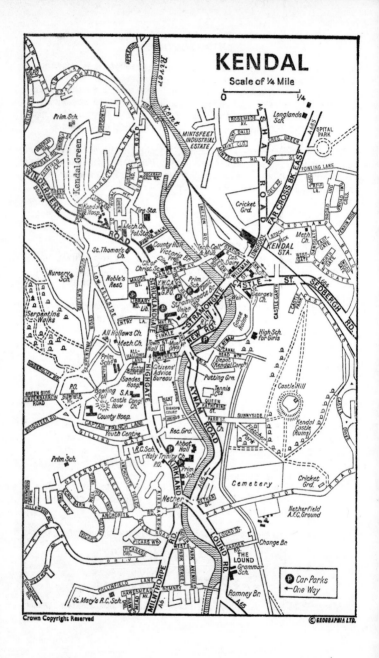

KENDAL

Scale of ¼ Mile

Car Parks
One Way

© GEOGRAPHIA LTD.

KENDAL

Population: 21,600
Early Closing Day: Thursday
Market Day: Saturday
Tourist Information Centre: Town Hall, Highgate   🛏

KENDAL, PICTURESQUELY SITUATED in the valley of the Kent and surrounded by lofty fells, is the main gateway from the south. It lies on the A6 which was the main road between the north and south, but the M6 now by-passes it on the road to Carlisle and there is another by-pass to the west on the road to the lakes.

Kendal serves as a centre for the trade and industry of the district. The main industries are the manufacture of shoes, carpets, water turbines and pumps, laundry machinery and cards for wool and cotton. There are quarries and a lime works nearby. There are no heavy industries and the place is a good shopping centre. The River Kent flows through the town, adding to the charm of the place. The river is crossed by three fine stone bridges, a girder bridge, a suspension bridge and a footbridge.

First Earl

Kendal has a long and varied history. There are signs of an early British settlement at Castle How and of an important Roman station at Watercrook where a Roman altar, now in the British Museum, was discovered. A fragment of an ancient monumental cross in a window on the south side of the parish church is the sole remaining relic of Saxon days. After the Norman Conquest, William the Conqueror created Ivo de Taillebois the first Earl of Kendal. Catherine Parr, one of the wives of Henry VIII, was born in Kendal Castle.

Castle Dairy

The parish church, the fifth largest parish church in England, dates from 1232 and is unique in that it has five aisles. It is mainly Perpendicular and is somewhat squat in appearance, the western tower being eighty feet high. It contains a wealth of memorials and trophies. Within the tower are ten bells, the earliest of them is dated 1537. Kendal Castle, of Norman origin and now in ruins, lies to the east of the town. Castle Dairy, near the station, is one of Kendal's ancient houses. It is still inhabited and can be inspected on payment of a small fee. It is an interesting example of Tudor domestic architecture, being rebuilt in 1564. Some parts of it are, however, much older, the doorways date from the fourteenth century.

Mayor's Parlour

In the Mayor's Parlour is Catherine Parr's Book of Devotions. Purchased for £500 in 1936, this is the only surviving possession of the Queen. The Parlour also contains a valuable collection of relics of George Romney who spent his youthful years in the town where he was apprenticed to a local artist. After many years in London Romney returned to Kendal where he died in 1802. The contents of the Mayor's Parlour may be inspected on application at the Town Hall. The Town Hall possesses a fine carillon of bells upon which tunes are played several times each day.

From the Town Hall climb westwards up Beasts Bank to Brigsteer Road and along there to Stainbank Green Farm. A gateway on the right of the road leads along a well-marked footpath to a precipice (Scout Scar) in grey limestone, 600 feet high, from where there is a wonderful panorama of the surrounding country. An indicator gives the names of the various points and fells to be seen.

Abbot Hall

In the Kirkland is Abbot Hall. The present building dates from the eighteenth century and was built by John Carr, the foremost architect in the north at that time. The property was bought by Kendal Corporation in 1897 and the park opened to the public. In 1962 the Hall itself was opened as an Art Gallery, and now contains a very fine collection (much of it local work) of paintings and objets d'art.

In 1971 the stable block was opened as the Museum of Lakeland Life and Industry, and illustrates the changing life-style of ordinary Lakeland people. Two rooms, parlour and bedroom are furnished in the manner prevailing before the First World War. The exhibits exemplify the contrast between those times and the more comfortable life of today. This fascinating museum has now expanded into part of the nearby old Grammar School.

Hawes Bridge

This is a popular walk along the banks of the river. Turn south off the main Lancaster road at Wattsfield Farm, along a footpath by one of the most pleasant reaches of the river to Hawes Bridge, a favourite subject for photographers.

SIZERGH CASTLE

About three miles south of Kendal lies Sizergh Castle, the home of the Strickland family for 700 years and now the property of the National Trust. It has a great Tudor Hall, fine panellings and ceilings, grand furniture and works of art. The peel tower dates from about 1340.

Open certain days April to September.

In the same area is Levens Hall, an Elizabethan mansion with fine Topiary Gardens laid out in 1689. The house has fine plaster ceilings, leather panelling and beautiful carved oak chimney pieces. There is a collection of working steam engines in the grounds and a herd of rare deer roam the adjoining park. Open daily Easter to September.

PENRITH

Population: 11,200
Early Closing Day: Wednesday
Market Day: Tuesday
Tourist Information Centre: Robinson's School, Middlegate. 🛏

PENRITH IS THE NORTHERN GATEWAY to the Lake District; like Kendal, it stands on the M6 to the north with other roads converging on to it.

It is a town with a long history and is built on a site occupied by the Celts about 500 B.C. Several relics of this occupation can still be seen. One is 'Long Meg and her Daughters', a stone circle situated near Little Salkeld, a village six miles north-east of Penrith on the Langwathby bus route. This circle is about three hundred and fifty yards in circumference and contains sixty-six stones, the largest being Long Meg, eighteen feet high. Others are Mayborough, a great area encircled by an embankment of stones, and King Arthur's Round Table, a circular arena, probably a medieval tilting ground, both on the Pooley Bridge road about one and half miles from the town.

Giant's Thumb

During the long Roman occupation, Penrith was an important road junction and many relics including pottery and coins have been found in the neighbourhood. The oldest existing monument is the tenth-century 'Giant's Thumb' in St. Andrew's churchyard, a rose cross of A.D. 920 commemorating 'Owen Caesarius' who was King of Cumberland and held his court at Penrith.

The town was granted a Market Charter by Henry II in 1223 and

became the 'Royal Town of Penrith'; the original seal is still preserved
in the museum which adjoins the Town Hall and Library and
contains many relics and pictures of old Penrith.

Like many other border towns, the streets of Penrith were built
narrow in order to defend the town from the invading Scots, the
Market Square in the centre being a wide space.

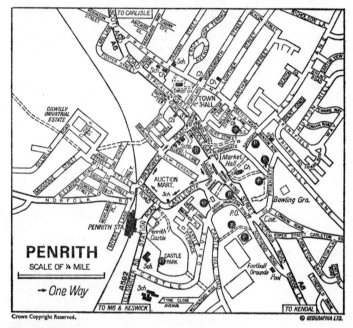

Crown Copyright Reserved.   © GEOGRAPHIA LTD.

The Castle

One of the principal attractions of Penrith is the old Castle, now
incorporated in the Castle Park, opposite the railway station. It was
built partly by Bishop Strickland and partly by the Nevilles, and was
occupied for some time by Richard III. In the north-east corner is
the remnant of Bishop Strickland's Tower, and in the vault below can
be seen some ancient stone cannonballs.

The courtyard shows the entire ground plan of the ancient building,
the basement walls standing above the level of the lawn. The grounds
now contain tennis courts, bowling green, putting course, children's
playground and a lovely rose garden. Band concerts are given in
the summer.

Parish Church

The parish church of St. Andrew is of very ancient foundation, records going back to 1133. The walls of the tower are six feet thick and on the north-west corner is a small ornament indicating the builder. It is the last of eight decorations on the top of the tower, each representing the arms of the Earls of Warwick, the bear and the ragged staff, and is testimony to the family connections with the town in the fourteenth and fifteenth centuries. The church suffered from fire and the nave was rebuilt in 1719. It has a fine peal of bells with a carillon attachment enabling hymn tunes to be played. The church contains many relics of the past, including some ancient inscribed coffin lids, while the many beautiful stained-glass windows include portraits of Richard III and his Queen.

Giant's Grave

In the churchyard is the Giant's Grave, supposed to be that of Owen Caesarius; it consists of two stone pillars standing at the head and foot of the grave fifteen feet apart. The two holes in the top of a nearby rose cross are said to be the size of his thumbs, hence its name, the Giant's Thumb.

Oldest House

Penrith possesses several ancient buildings. The Gloucester Arms Hotel in Great Dockray was once the residence of Richard III: its rooms are panelled in very old black oak. In the same street is the Two Lions Hotel, dating back to 1585, the ceiling of the dining-room is covered with geometric designs in plaster work, the centre of each incorporating a coat-of-arms. Part of the Tudor Café, overlooking the parish churchyard, is a little old red sandstone house built in 1563, the oldest house in Penrith.

Penrith Beacon

The outstanding feature of the surroundings is Penrith Beacon and Pike. This can be easily reached from the town on foot by way of Sandgate and Fell Lane. Then opposite where the latter joins Beacon Road a footpath leads to the top of the Pike. It is 937 feet above sea-level and the view from the top includes Saddleback, the Vale of Eden, Ullswater, the Pennines, and the Scottish hills over the Solway.

The Pike

The Pike, a pointed stone building, was erected only in 1719, but Penrith Beacon had been lighted many times before this. The Pike was used for the 1745 Rising, and the last record is of 1804, during the Napoleonic Wars, when it warned Sir Walter Scott to return to Scotland to join the Regiment of Volunteers, of which he was a member.

BROUGHAM CASTLE

Brougham Castle, now in ruins, stands one and a half miles south-east of Penrith. It is reached by leaving the town by the Appleby road, then down Frenchfield Avenue. The castle was held by the Viteriponts and De Cliffords. James I was a guest there at one time. The outer walls of the castle are still in a state of fair preservation. It is open to the public from 10 a.m. to 7 p.m. on weekdays and 2 p.m. to 7 p.m. on Sundays, closing earlier in the winter months. The castle can be visited by bus on the Appleby and Crosby Ravensworth routes.

A pleasant walk can be enjoyed by continuing a mile beyond the castle along Brougham Avenue Road, then by Lowther Bridge to Eamont Bridge and by the Skirgill fields into Penrith.

LOWTHER CASTLE

Take the Shap bus to Hackthorpe. Turn right through Lowther village then through the gateway past the Lowther Estate Office into the castle grounds. The road passes in front of the castle, affording a fine view of the building which was the largest and most handsome between the Ribble and the Border. The castle used to be the residence of Lord Lonsdale, and during that time he would

Lowther Castle

occasionally throw parts of it open to the public. It was sometimes visited by Royalty and more than once the German Emperor has stayed there. The castle was demolished a few years ago and only the shell remains. Part of the grounds is now a Wild Life picnic park containing a number of rare birds and animals. Open May to September.

Nearby is the church, the churchyard containing the mausoleum of the Lowthers. The walk can be continued to the quaint village of Askham and the return to Penrith is made by bus.

ST. NINIAN'S CHURCH

To visit this ancient place take the Appleby bus to Brougham Bridge. On alighting, continue along the road about a third of a mile, and a stone pillar on the right commemorates the parting of the Countess of Pembroke and her mother, the Countess of Cumberland. This four-sided pillar is something of a rarity, one side contains an ancient sundial. Half a mile beyond, a signpost on the left directs you through some fields to St. Ninian's Church, by the side of the River Eamont, a walk of sheer beauty. Return by bus.

KIRKOSWALD

The charming village of Kirkoswald, nine miles north-east of Penrith, has a very interesting old church which was founded centuries before the Norman Conquest; the belfry is placed away on a hill a short distance from the church. A short distance away are the ruins of Kirkoswald Castle, founded in the thirteenth century by Randolph Engayne, and once one of the finest mansions in the North of England.

GRANGE OVER SANDS

Population: 3,650
Early Closing Day: Thursday
Tourist Information Centre: Victoria Hall, Main Street   🛏️

ALTHOUGH NOT SUCH A POPULAR GATEWAY to the Lakes as Penrith and Kendal, Grange-over-Sands is within easy reach, Windermere Lake at Newby Bridge being only seven miles away on a regular bus route.

Grange-over-Sands is worth visiting for it is one of the loveliest spots on the Lakeland coast. Situated in Morecambe Bay, on a clear day Morecambe and even Blackpool can be seen across the Bay, and in the summer swimming contests are arranged across the Bay between Hest Bank and Grange.

Fine Gardens

The town is noted for its woodlands and gardens. Near to the station is an ornamental and sunken garden with an artificial lake which provides a feast of beauty, even tropical trees flourish there and the yucca tree is often admired. Wild fowl occupy the lake. In the Park Road Gardens, Sunday band concerts are given in the season. It contains a fine rose garden.

The Promenade is over a mile in length and bedecked with

rockeries and flower-beds. It is a delightful walk at full tide and
rowing-boats may be hired. On the Promenade is the open-air
bathing pool filled with sea water. In size it is 165 feet by 112 feet
and is well supplied with diving-boards and chute. The depth varies
from ten feet to one and half feet. It contains an up-to-date café,
sunbathing terraces and a paddling pool for children.

Hampsfell Hospice

This square building stands on Hampsfell and was erected by the
Rev. Thomas Remington as a shelter for wanderers over the fell.
From its elevation of 750 feet it overlooks Morecambe Bay and
commands an extensive view including Black Combe, the Coniston
Fells, Langdales, Scafell, Helvellyn and the Pennines. It is reached by
climbing Hampsfell Road out of Grange.

Woodland Beauty

Egerslack Wood lies off the Windermere road and in spring and
summer is a fairyland of woodland beauty. It contains some
interesting specimens of flora and fauna. The pathway through the
wood can be followed on to Hampsfell.

Holker Hall

Holker Hall, five miles from Grange, dates from the sixteenth
century, with later additions. The interior has a wealth of wood
carving and a magnificent stairway. The spacious library contains
some 3,500 books. Many exotic flowering trees and bushes,
including a very old Tulip tree, deer and sheep, are to be seen in the
twenty-two acres of garden and park land. There are excellent
catering facilities and a gift shop. The Hall is open daily except
Saturdays, from Easter to the end of September.

CARTMEL PRIORY

The village of Cartmel can be reached by bus or by walking two
miles over Hampsfell. It is chiefly visited for its great priory church.
It was originally the church of an Augustinian priory founded early
in the reign of Richard I. It is a noble building, mainly in the
Transitional Norman style of the late twelfth century, though the
nave is Perpendicular as is also the magnificent east window. The
tower is unique in having its upper portion placed diagonally on the
original Norman section. There are many interesting features in the
church, chief of which are the extraordinary carvings on the early
fifteenth-century misericords, the Harrington tomb, a huge parochial
umbrella reputed to be over two hundred years old and an extensive
library of early theological books.

Section 3   Principal Centres

KESWICK

Population: 5,000
Early Closing Day: Wednesday
Market Day: Saturday
Tourist Information and National Park Centre: Moot Hall,
  Market Square and Council Offices, 50 Main Street

KESWICK IS THE UNDISPUTED HUB of the Lake District; by
means of bus services, any part of the Lake District can be reached
with ease in a very short time. From no other centre of Lakeland are
so many lakes and such a variety of fell walks so readily accessible.
Keswick's veritable girdle of fells, which include Skiddaw, Saddleback, Helvellyn, Scafell, Robinson and Grisedale, has no equal.

Pleasant Centre
   Those who wish to see the beauties of Lakeland in the most
expeditious and easiest way will find Keswick the best centre, and

in addition its setting is in one of the loveliest spots in the kingdom. The town itself is a clean, pleasant place with fine shops catering for the visitors, and Derwentwater, the queen of the lakes, is about ten minutes' walk from the town.

The weekly market, a charter for which was granted by Edward I in 1276, is held on Saturday.

One-handed clock

The old Moot Hall in the Market Square was erected in 1813, and has one of the oldest one-handed clocks, which is a continued source of interest and speculation. In the tower of the Hall hangs a bell bearing the date 1601 and the letters H.D.R.O., which is said to have come from the ancestral home of the Derwentwaters on Lord's Isle.

The original Parish Church is at Crosthwaite, about half a mile out of Keswick in the direction of Cockermouth. It was built in 1553 on the site of a much earlier church and is dedicated to St. Kentigern. This sixth-century Bishop of Glasgow (known there as St. Mungo) fled from the pagan ruler, Morken, to this 'thwaite', or clearing, where he raised his 'cross'. The church was restored in 1845, and contains a fourteenth-century font and a fine recumbent effigy of Southey, who lived for forty years at the nearby Greta Hall, was made Poet Laureate in 1813, and is buried in the churchyard.

Sir Hugh Walpole

St. John's Church is a more modern building on the edge of the town and its spire is a prominent landmark. From its terraced walk there is a delightful view of meadow, wood, lake and fell, with Brandelhow and Silver Hill beyond the lake covered with bushy foliage up to the bracken-clad slopes of Catbells and Maidenmoor. Sir Hugh Walpole, the famous Lakeland author, lies buried in the churchyard overlooking the lake.

The Public Library in Tithe Barn Street is open to visitors. The Keswick High School of Industrial Arts is at High Hill. Here all kinds of hand-worked art in silver, copper, brass, and other metals can be inspected and bought.

Just outside the former railway station is a small but interesting Museum which specializes in souvenirs, MSS. and portraits of Lake poets. It has also a good collection of local birds, minerals, and a 3-inch-to-the-mile relief model of the Lake District.

Keswick is famous for the excellence of its lead pencils, being the birthplace of the industry. In the vicinity of the town are many old mines and quarries. Copper, lead and other metallic ores have been wrested from the mines, the majority of which are now derelict,

Kirkstone Pass   Towards Brotherswater

Ravenglass & Eskdale   Miniature Railway

Lake Windermere   The "Swan"

while the quarries provide materials which are the admiration of roadmakers, architects, and builders; Honister slate is considered the finest in the country.

Among the most attractive features of Keswick are the High and Low Fitz Parks through which flows the River Greta, coming from Thirlmere. There are bowls and tennis and pleasant walks amidst beautiful surroundings in the High Park, while in the Low Park are swings and seesaws for the children, also tennis courts and facilities for cricket and football.

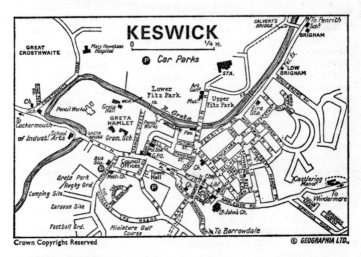

DERWENTWATER

Queen of the lakes, and most beautiful, Derwentwater is three miles long, just over one mile wide and is very shallow at each end. It owes its beauty to its many islands, the rich blending of the surrounding steep crags and green fells, and the beautifully wooded shores. The lake contains three large islands, all abundantly wooded with the foliage of the trees dropping down to the water's edge. The largest is Derwent Isle, opposite the landing stage; there is a large house on this island which is private property. The other two wooded islands are Lord's Island, opposite Friar's Crag, and St. Herbert's Island, in the middle of the lake. There is a smaller island, Rampsholme Island, nearer the eastern shore, and the Floating Island near Lodore, which appears at infrequent intervals. The motor launches which sail round the lake in both directions call at Barrow House Landing (near Watendlath Road end), Lodore, High

C

Brandelhow, Low Brandelhow and Hawes End. A trip round the lake takes about an hour and is very pleasant.

AROUND KESWICK

Route 1: FRIAR'S CRAG. One of the most popular rendezvous for the visitor is Friar's Crag, about twenty minutes' walk from the centre of the town. Leave the Market Square by the Borrowdale road and turn right into Lake Road, past the miniature golf links to the boat landings. The busy Lake Road can be avoided by continuing a short distance along the Borrowdale road beyond the top of Lake Road and turning down a narrow walk signposted to the Lake. Another route from the town is through St. John's churchyard, across the road and down the pedestrian track to the lake.

The walk along the road above the boat landings is one of great beauty. Leaving the landings, the track passes through a gate into a charming wood, and a short distance along is the small, prominent Friar's Crag which gives the best marginal view of Derwentwater. After heavy rain the waters of Lodore Falls can be both seen and heard from this point. Friar's Crag is so named because it was the landing-place of the friars of Grange.

On the crag is the Ruskin Monument, erected in 1900, a simple block of Borrowdale stone bearing on one side a bronze medallion portrait, with the inscription beneath: 'The first thing that I remember as an event in life was being taken by my nurse to the brow of Friar's Crag, Derwentwater.' On the other side is a Celtic cross with the inscription: 'The spirit of God is around you in the air you breathe, His glory in the light you see, and in the fruitfulness of the earth and the joys of His creatures. He has written for you day by day His revelation, and He has granted you day by day your daily bread.'

The whole of this area, including Friar's Crag, Lord's Island and Scarf Close Bay, was acquired by the National Trust in 1921 as a memorial to Canon Rawnsley, one of the founders of the Trust, and a memorial tablet lies alongside the walk on to the Crag. Since then, the whole of the shore around Derwentwater has been given to or bought for the Trust and is open to the public.

The walk can be continued by the lake shore, through a gate, and by a field into a wood. Keep to the track, which is well marked. Turn right on emerging from the wood on to a road, and right again at the second gate, passing to the left of a farm, then by the shore again to Broomhill Point, not unlike Friar's Crag in appearance. After following the shore for a short distance beyond Broomhill Point, by Scarf Close Bay, the track rises at several points to join the main Borrowdale road, about a mile from Keswick. There is a good footpath on the opposite side of the hedge from the road for much of the distance between Ashness Road end and Keswick.

Route 2: CASTLE HEAD. One of the finest viewpoints, for its altitude, in the Lake District. The usual entrance is a small opening about a quarter of a mile along the Borrowdale road on the left side of the road. There is a short, sharp climb to the summit, 300 feet high, from where all your energies will be rewarded. An alternative route is to proceed to the foot of Manor Brow, then along Springs Road. Near the end, a narrow fenced track goes to the right to the foot of Castle Head. The climb up through the wood to the summit is rather easier than from the Borrowdale road. The whole of Derwentwater lies beneath in all its beauty with Catbells, Maiden Moor, Causey Pike and Grisedale Pike in the background. To the right of the lake is Bassenthwaite Lake, with Skiddaw on the right. Beyond Bassenthwaite it may be possible to see Criffell, one of the Scottish hills in Kirkcudbrightshire. Turning farther right, Saddleback, then part of the Helvellyn range comes into view, while closer at hand in the same direction is Walla Crag, which overlooks Derwentwater. To the left of the lake is Borrowdale, with the steep pyramidal rock called Castle Crag, nearly 1,000 feet high, which forms part of the jaws of Borrowdale

Route 3: CASTLERIGG STONE CIRCLE. Start along the Penrith road by taking the road from the Memorial opposite the County Hotel. The road follows the river for some distance, then rises over the railway. Keep left at the first fork and right at the second, which is the old Penrith-Keswick road. This rises for about half a mile, and at the top the Circle will be found in a field adjoining the road, indicated by a stile, near the east corner of a narrow lane on the right side. The tall stones of this ancient monument describe a circle nearly a hundred feet in diameter. It commands an extensive and magnificent view, standing in the centre of an immense girdle of fells with a panoramic view of nearly a hundred miles in circumference It includes Saddleback. Skiddaw, Helvellyn, Scafell, Grisedale Pike and many other of the highest fells.

The return journey may be made by continuing the walk along Castle Lane to join the Ambleside road about two miles from Keswick.

Alternatively, take a Ribble bus to Rakefoot Road end, then follow signposts.

Route 4: BARROW FALLS. Follow the path and road along the east side of Derwentwater to just beyond Barrow Landing.

This fine fall of over 100 feet is a little over two miles from Keswick and lies immediately behind Barrow House, now a Youth Hostel.

It is near here that the Floating Island appears at intervals.

Alternatively, take the Borrowdale bus from Market Square to Barrow House, or a motor launch to Barrow landing.

Route 5: LODORE FALLS. Follow the path and road on the east side of Derwentwater to the Lodore Hotel.

Alternatively, take the Borrowdale bus from Market Square to Lodore Hotel, or a motor launch to Lodore landing.

The Lodore Falls lie about four miles from Keswick and are a very popular excursion. Although Southey's famous poem exaggerates slightly the grandeur of the Lodore Falls, his clever rhyming paints a wonderful picture of the tumbling waters every word of which does become true after heavy rain when the cataracts are in full spate. The poet begins quietly, describing its origins:

> 'From its sources which well
> In the Tarn on the fell;
> From its fountains
> In the mountains
> Its rills and its gills . . .'

Thereafter the tumbling adjectives, skilfully rhymed, convey the progress of the water down the rocks:

> 'Writhing and ringing
> Eddying and whisking
> Spouting and frisking,
> Turning and twisting . . .'

Then, after many more lines in which he catches the gathering majesty and power of the rushing water, the poet describes how it descends finally:

> 'And so never ending, but always descending
> Sounds and motions for ever and ever are blending,
> All at once and all o'er, with a mighty uproar,
> And this way the waters come down at Lodore.'

Route 6/7: RAKEFOOT, CASTLERIGG. Start up St. John's Street past St. John's Church to the foot of Manor Brow, turn right to Springs Farm, and then up the hill by the side of the stream which is crossed by a wooden bridge. Pass through a gate and turn right along a road past Rakefoot Farm, cross a river, and a footpath ascends the hill with a beck on the left, over a wooden ladder stile, then keep right to the summit cairn on Walla Crag. There is a very extensive view from here.

Those who wish to keep on good ground should return along the same route to Rakefoot, but those who do not mind a bit of rough land can continue along the crags on to Falcon Crag, then drop down the fell side to join the Watendlath road just below Ashness Bridge, then follow either the road or lake shore to Keswick or return by bus from the road end, or launch from the landing. A new attractive footpath starts on the right just below Ashness Bridge, goes along the fell side over a stile: keep right to Great Wood, ascend by the side of it, cross a beck and descend to a car park in the wood. Leave this by the exit on the left, cross the main road and follow the footpath by lake shore by Broom Point and Friars Crag to Keswick, 3 miles from Ashness Bridge. There is also a short but very steep, rough descent from the summit of Walla Crag by a path which starts over a stile in the Borrowdale direction, and descends by a steep ghyll. At the bottom there is a very pleasant walk through a wood towards Keswick which joins the road in about half a mile. *(Easy to Walla Crag, fairly easy right round.) Walla Crag 3 miles. Complete walk 6½ miles.*

Route 8: HIGH SEAT. Follow Route 6/7 on to Walla Crag, then make for the ruined Lodge a short distance away, and follow the course of a dried-up beck round the right of Castlerigg Fell (in wet weather this may be boggy), then ascend to the left to Ashness Ghyll. Cross the ghyll below a small nob and make for the summit cairn on Ashness Fell. The summit of High Seat can now be seen, and the best way is to proceed directly to it. There is a view of Thirlmere from the summit, behind which is the Helvellyn range; Pike o' Stickle can be seen to the south.

Return down the fell, keeping Ashness Ghyll on your right until a good footpath appears which leads down to Ashness Bridge and the road back to Keswick. The bus can be taken to Keswick from the main road. *9 miles. (Moderate.)*

Route 9: GALE ROAD. Leave Keswick by the Lower Market Place, over Greta Bridge, then turn right along the main road to Carlisle. Follow this for about half a mile, turn up a right hand road for about half a mile to join Gale Road, then right up hill. The road, originally used by Romans on their travels from the west coast to the east, rises through beautiful country for about a mile. From the top of the hill where the road ends, a worthwhile diversion is to the top of Latrigg for the wonderful view, keep to the right of the fence as you ascend. From the top proceed in the direction of Saddleback, cross a wooden stile and continue along a cart track towards Derwentfolds Farm, joining the Brundholme Park road near a road fork.

From the top of Gale Road you can either turn right through a gate to descend Spoony Green Lane to Keswick or continue round the side of Latrigg, dropping down to the Glenderaterra Beck above Brundholme, then by the road which leads through Brundholme Woods, with delightful views of the River Greta below. Take the second road on the left, about 2 miles from Brundholme, which crosses the river to join the main road into Keswick. *6 miles. (Easy.)*

Route 10: APPLETHWAITE TERRACE. Follow Route 9 as far as the junction with Gale Road, then continue down the hill to Applethwaite. A little farther on is the small house of prayer and soon comes Millbeck, once a busy little village where there were several woollen mills. For over a century the wheels were turned by the little stream which races down the fell side. Below is Millbeck Hall, a quaint old building built around a 'Peel Tower', at one time the home of the Williamsons. The road then joins the main road which leads back to Keswick. *6 miles. (Easy.)*

Route 11: A WALK ROUND DERWENTWATER. Leave Keswick by the Cockermouth road; immediately after crossing Greta Bridge turn left to follow the footpath to Portinscale (the walk can be shortened by taking the Cockermouth bus from Keswick Bus Station to Portinscale).

Turn down the road on the left and follow this for about half a mile, or ten minutes' walking. Immediately after passing Derwent Bank, the Holiday Fellowship Guest House, turn left through a sign-posted gap and follow a footpath which rises up through Silver Hill Wood to Lingholme. The path passes to the right of the drive to the house, through a field, and into another wood, emerging from this on to a narrow road. Turn left along this road for about ten yards, then through a footgate on the left, drop down to the lake shore. The path now follows the shore past Low Brandelhow Pier, through Brandelhow Park to High Brandelhow Pier. After crossing a stile, the path drops to the lake again, passes in front of a house and turns left. It continues through the fields, coming near the water edge in parts, round Great Bay, and crosses some swampy ground by wooden boards raised above the ground. In wet weather this land is often under water and impassable. Crossing the river by a bridge, the main road is reached, and turning left along here it is a short distance to Lodore Hotel, behind which are the famous falls. *Distance right round 10 miles. (Easy.)*

Route 12: WATENDLATH. Take the Borrowdale bus from Market Square to Watendlath Road end. By launch to Barrow landing, or by walking either along the main road or from Great Wood car park by the footpath to Ashness Bridge to avoid road walking.

This is one of the most popular walks in the district, involving little climbing, and the views are magnificent. Start from Watendlath Road end; from the gate the road rises fairly sharply for a half-mile until it comes to the famous Ashness Bridge, a favourite haunt of artists; here is the first of several views of Derwentwater, Bassenthwaite and Skiddaw.

A short distance along the road is a wooden hut, and a path to the right leads to a second viewpoint overlooking Derwentwater. The

road next passes a house, rises through a field and enters another
wood, and a few yards inside this wood a path to the right leads on to
Gowder Crag, the third and probably the finest viewpoint of all. The
main road at Lodore lies many hundreds of feet below at the foot of
the cliff, and the cars and boats look like mere toys.

About 500 yards along the road, a green lane signposted to
Watendlath starts on the right. Cross the first wooden stile on the left
(the track straight on leads to Lodore Hotel), this leads down an
attractive lane to a second stile where you join a path coming down
from the Watendlath road. Turn right down this path and cross the
Watendlath Beck by a wooden bridge. There is a stone signpost in the
ground. Turn left and follow the right-hand bank of the river for
about 1½ miles to Watendlath, a charming hamlet made famous by
Sir Hugh Walpole in his 'Rogue Herries' books. Just below the
hamlet is a pretty waterfall known as the Devil's Punchbowl.

The wooden bridge over Watendlath Beck can also be reached
from the main road by a path which starts by High Lodore Farm on
the Keswick side of Borrowdale Hotel, it zig-zags up Ladder Brow
where a close view may be obtained of climbers on Shepherds'
Crag, the most popular climbing venue in Borrowdale. From the first

The Bowder Stone

stile up the hill a ten-minute diversion from the path to the top of Shepherds' Crag is worth-while for the extensive view. Continue up your original path which crosses another stile, turns right, and passes through a gate to reach the footbridge.

Watendlath hamlet is reached by crossing the old pack-horse bridge at the foot of Watendlath Tarn. To continue this walk, return over the bridge and follow a path which skirts the edge of the tarn for a few yards before rising sharply for about a quarter of a mile. Continue along the top for a short distance, then the pony track drops towards Rosthwaite. A grand view of the upper Borrowdale Valley, with Honister Pass, Dale Head, Great Gable and Glaramara is obtained as you descend to Rosthwaite.

To reach the Bowder Stone, unless you particularly wish to reach Rosthwaite, the shortest route is to take the first or preferably the second path which starts at a gap in the wall on the right, about half way down the fellside. Both descend diagonally down the fellside. through a wood, to join the main road below. Turning right along the road, take the next fork to the right, through a gate, to the Bowder Stone. A road from the Stone leads down to join the main road about ten minutes' walk away, and the return to Keswick may be made by bus. *Distance to Bowder Stone via Watendlath from Keswick, 10 miles. (Moderate.)*

Route 13: KING'S HOW. This is a very neglected fell, which is surprising as it is an easy climb and commands a grand view of Derwentwater in all its beauty, together with Helvellyn, Fairfield and the Borrowdale fells.

Take the Borrowdale bus from Market Square to Grange and, about 100 yards from the road end in the direction of Seatoller, cross a stile on the left with the National Trust sign naming Grange Fell at the side. A footpath runs due east round the foot of the towering crags of King's How, and forks at about half-mile just before reaching a stile. Follow the right fork, which crosses a beck, then rises up through a wood in a fairly sharp but easy ascent; nearby on the left you follow a beck for a while, then the path swings to the right and is quite easy to follow as it is marked by cairns near the top.

Grange Fell and the Borrowdale Birches, consisting of 310 acres, was purchased in 1910 as a memorial to King Edward VII, handed over to the National Trust and named King's How. Near the summit is a slab of Borrowdale slate bearing the inscription:

> 'Here may all beings gather strength and
> Find in scenes of beautiful nature a cause
> for gratitude and love to God giving them
> Courage and vigour to carry on His will.

The return journey may be either by the path you have just climbed, or by another path from the summit in the direction of Borrowdale. From the first wall a path drops rather steeply to join the main road by a stile just beyond the Bowder Stone. *Grange to King's How and Bowder Stone, 2 miles. (Moderate.)*

Route 14: LOBSTONE BAND, MAIDEN MOOR, CAT BELLS. By Seatoller bus to Rosthwaite. Opposite Rosthwaite Post Office, turn down a narrow road on your right (facing Seatoller) which leads to the river, crossed by a bridge. The way then rises up the fell side to some old workings (slate quarries). Beyond that is a rough foot track leading to the summit of Lobstone Band. Turn right along a footpath which rises to the top of Scawdel Fell; a large cairn marks the summit. To the left is Eel Crags; when looked at from above, few precipices in the district have a more formidable appearance than these. There is a fine mountain panorama and practically all the major Lakeland fells can be seen.

The route is now along a pony track, easy to follow, as it drops to Maiden Moor by Narrow Moor, with magnificent views of Derwentwater meeting you in many places. The track later drops off Maiden Moor, crosses a track between Little Town and Manesty, and then rises over Cat Bells, along a rather narrow ridge walk, still more grand views, before finally descending sharply to join the road near to Hawse End. By walking down to the lake, the launch can be caught at Hawse End Pier for Keswick. *7 miles. (Moderate.)*

Route 15: SKIDDAW. This walk starts from Keswick, passing through Low Fitz Park, past the houses to cross the A66 by a footbridge. Then join a rough unmetalled track, Spoony Green Lane, which starts from the road on the right. Continue up here for a good half-hour's easy walking until, at the top, it joins another track coming up from Gale.

Higher up, pass through a gate on the right, turn left along a fenced path with a plantation (recently partly felled) on your right, and cross over a stile on to open fell land. There is now a long climb up Jenkin Hill. From the top of the hill there is quite a good pony track rising at an easy gradient to the summit of Skiddaw, which is Lakeland's fourth highest mountain, 3,054 feet high.

The view from the summit includes the whole of Derwentwater, the Solway, with Scotland and the Isle of Man beyond. Many of the popular fells are to be seen, but the view in this respect cannot compare with that of many other peaks at a lower level.

Almost due east is Skiddaw Forest, though little remains except a square plantation with some derelict cottages nearby. To return to Keswick by a different route from the ascent, you can drop down the fell side to this plantation, and then either turn left along the

cart road which will lead past Dash Falls, one of the lesser-known
Lakeland falls, and on to Bassenthwaite village where you can
obtain a bus back from Castle Inn to Keswick, or you can turn right
and the track will lead round Lonscale Fell, down the right of
Glenderaterra Beck, by a rough footpath which eventually leads back
to the track by which you ascended, joining it at the foot of Jenkin
Hill, then continue down Spoony Green Lane back to Keswick. Be
careful not to descend north-eastwards into the tangled mass of
lower fells on either side of the River Caldew. It is especially
undesirable to get lost here in misty weather as the walker can tramp
for several miles without coming on a single house or farm.
10 miles. (Moderate.)

Route 16: LONSCALE. This is another neglected fell, and the
view from the top is much superior to that from Skiddaw, although
Lonscale is only 2,344 feet high.

Follow the route described in the previous walk up Spoony Green
Lane to the top of Jenkin Hill. At the top, pass through a gate, then
immediately turn right along a wire fence; cross this fence about
one hundred yards along, and make for the top of Lonscale Fell,
about two minutes' walk.

The best viewpoint is the top of a crag about one hundred yards
east of the summit from where the full length of Thirlmere can be
seen with a portion of Coniston Water behind it. There is also a
good view of Derwentwater and many of the fells, the Helvellyn
range being especially prominent.

From the crag, walk along the edge to the left for some two
hundred yards until it is possible to drop down the fell side to a
footpath observed below coming from a stone wall. This path leads
under the crag on which you were standing, then drops again to
join the footpath along the fell side to the right of Glenderaterra
Beck. This path leads to Spoony Green Lane and Keswick.

This is a much easier walk than Skiddaw. *7 miles (Moderate.)*

Route 17: SADDLEBACK (or Blencathra). Take the Penrith or
Patterdale bus to Scales. A footpath starts behind the White Horse
Inn, and rises sharply for a short distance after which there is an easy
gradient. Follow this footpath for about a mile and a half; after the
first half-mile the Glendermackin Beck flows on the right.

At the point where a fast-flowing beck crosses the track, climb
up the hillside on the left, keeping the beck on your right until you
reach Scales Tarn, five to ten minutes' walk upstream. You have now
an alternative route. For the more cautious, the route winds round
the fell side on the left of the tarn; there is no well-defined footpath,
but by making for the top of the fell it is impossible to go wrong.

The more interesting route, however, is by Sharp Edge; this narrow ledge, not unlike Striding Edge on Helvellyn, is only about a foot wide in parts, and on either side are steep mountain slopes or crags. Taken with care, in good weather it is quite safe. It should NOT be attempted in wild or misty weather, or when covered with snow and ice. Inexperienced fell walkers should be roped together for safety.

To climb by Sharp Edge, leave the Tarn at its outlet and climb up the grassy slope due north. The path soon reaches the narrow ledge and those who keep to the edge will find some exciting scrambling. It is not very far across, and soon the edge widens out to a steep scree slope which the inexperienced may find difficult; care is required. Higher up, it widens out to a grassy slope, and a few yards farther the summit of Saddleback is reached.

The view includes the full length of Thirlmere, St. John's in the Vale, Derwentwater, the Helvellyn range, and the many fells west and south of Derwentwater.

The route now lies across the top of the fell in the direction of Derwentwater; there are many fine ridges below, some not unlike Sharp Edge, but not as sharp. Passing Knowe Crags, the fell opens out into a wide grassy slope; a farm, Derwentfolds, will be seen in the bottom, and this is the next objective. To the left of the farm is a hostel belonging to the Planning Board. From the farm a lane drops down to cross Glenderaterra Beck, and then follows a pleasant walk through Brundholme Woods, with views of the River Greta below, to Keswick. *7 miles. (Fairly strenuous.)*

Route 18: GRISEDALE PIKE, CAUSEY PIKE. Take the Cockermouth bus to Braithwaite (some run only to Braithwaite). After alighting proceed up the road in the direction of Whinlatter Pass, and at the bottom of the fell, in between the angle formed by Whinlatter and Coledale Passes, climb the well-worn footpath up the fell side to Kinn. The first hundred yards is very steep, but after that the gradient eases and should present no difficulty. The path is well marked as it leads up to Grisedale Pike. Next follows an interesting ridge walk across Sand Hill, from where you can look down the valley deep below Hobcarton Crags.

The path drops to Sand Hill, then begins to rise again to Hobcarton Pike; drop down the fell side from Sand Hill towards a beck observed coming off Grasmoor, the fell across the immediate valley. Climb up the left side of the beck for a short distance, then the path crosses the beck, and you can either bear right to the summit of Grasmoor, or keep left along a small valley between Grasmoor and Eel Crags to Wandope.

From the top of Grasmoor is a splendid view of Loweswater, Crummock and Buttermere, a better view of Crummock is obtained by walking a few yards west. To continue, proceed due east from the summit and bear right slightly until you reach the ridge coming

up off Wandope. The track rises sharply, with a valley deep below
on the right, to the top of Eel Crags, another grand viewpoint. Next
is an unmistakable ridge walk over Sail on to Causey Pike, then
follows a sharp descent to the valley below. Join the road, cross the
Newlands Beck at Stair and follow the road either to Portinscales
and Keswick, or to Hawes End Pier for the launch to Keswick.
12 miles. (Strenuous).

Route 19: DALE HEAD AND ROBINSON. By bus to Braithwaite.
Turn left at the Inn, crossing the river by a stone bridge. Pass through
the next gate on the right to a house where there is a sign marked
'Footpath'. Continue along this until it reaches the main Newlands
road. In about a third of a mile turn down a signposted lane on the
left, past Uzzicar, through a gate on your left at the farm, until you
reach Newlands Beck, a path on the left of the Beck leads to
Stair, then by a narrow country road to Littletown. (Taking the
mini-bus from Keswick to Stair shortens the route by about three
miles.) Where the road drops towards Newlands church, follow a
track on the left which goes up the valley to the left of Newlands
Beck. Later the track becomes a path and rises sharply until it reaches
Dale Head Tarn at the top.
     There is a fairly steep and rough climb in a westerly direction;
up the fell side from the Tarn to the ridge; a cairn marks the summit
of Dale Head. There is a fine view of the valley through which you
have just come, and of Great Gable and Scafell in the opposite
direction.
     Robinson, which is the next objective, can be observed to the west,
and the route from here is along an interesting ridge walk, with a wire
fence serving as a good guide all the way. Leave the fence just before
reaching Robinson and the summit is a short distance on the right.
The view includes Loweswater, Crummock and Buttermere, and by
walking a few yards east, Derwentwater comes into view.
     Continuing east, the path from Robinson drops to the right of
some crags down High Snab Bank to Newlands church, and the
route of the outward journey can now be retraced to Braithwaite.
It is a delightful walk, embracing many fine views. This route may
be shortened if desired by turning off Robinson in the direction of
Buttermere Lake. A short way down is a flat piece of land, Buttermere Moss, and the footpath goes across the centre, bears right to
the edge, then descends in a direct line for Buttermere village, seen
below. *14 miles. (Strenuous.)*

Route 20: LORD'S SEAT. By Cockermouth bus via Braithwaite
to the Swan Hotel. Opposite the hotel, a track leaves the road to cross
Beckstones Ghyll, then turns right, crosses a wooden fence and rises
up through a plantation. At the top it comes on to open fell; cross

the fence on the right and follow this to the summit of Lord's Seat. The view includes the Solway coast, the lower end of Bassenthwaite, and a good panorama of the fells.

A better view is obtained by taking the footpath on the right from the top of the plantation for a diversion on to Barf, lower than Lord's Seat, but a more extensive viewpoint.

An interesting descent is to proceed west along a ridge to Broom Fell, a broken wall marks the summit, then descend N.W. towards a footpath which can be observed below to the left of Burthwaite Heights. This leads down the valley by Tom Rudd Beck to a stone bridge. Turn left up the road for about 50 yards, then right down a lane, over a wooden bridge, down to Embleton church. Pass through the churchyard, and a path leads through some fields to Embleton station (now closed), where the bus can be taken back to Keswick. *7 miles. (Fairly strenuous.)*

FOREST TRAILS

There are two interesting Forest Trails at Bassenthwaite. One starts near the Swan Hotel at Thornthwaite and follows a signposted lane to the lake. By taking the left-hand gate at the twin gates before reaching the lake, an enjoyable walk through Pow Howe Woods will lead back to the start near to the Swan Hotel.

The second Forest Trail starts at Little Crosthwaite, on the main Castle Inn–Keswick road through Dodd Wood: a short guide to the walk is available near the entrance. There is a choice of three routes, short, medium (Forest Trail), and long. The latter takes you to the top of Dodd Fell where there is an extensive view over Derwentwater, Borrowdale, Newlands, and the whole of Bassenthwaite Lake, a view well worth the short climb.

A Forestry Commission Leisure Centre at the summit of Whinlatter Pass has an information room and exhibition. A guide map to the vicinity is on sale in the Centre.

TOURS FROM KESWICK

The following tours are, unless otherwise stated, suitable for both motorists and cyclists.

Tour 4. Borrowdale road as far as Grange, turn right over the twin bridge, along the side of Cat Bells to Portinscale, back to Keswick. *9 miles.*

Tour 5. Down the main street over Greta Bridge, turn right along the Carlisle road as far as the crossroads at Castle Inn, keep left from here, past Amathwaite Hall to Ouse Bridge at the foot of Bassenthwaite Lake, turn left over bridge and follow lake side road which joins the A66 at Dub Wath. Follow this back to Keswick. *18 miles.*

Tour 6. Penrith road to Threlkeld, turn right past the old disused station, down the Vale of St. Johns, along Thirlmere, turn right at the end of the lake (head) to complete a circle of Thirlmere, back to Keswick. *16 miles.*

Tour 7. Main road by Bassenthwaite Lake to Cockermouth (cyclists should take the secondary road by turning left at the Pheasant Hotel, Bassenthwaite Lake, to Wythop Mill, joining the main road five miles beyond the hotel. The road is suitable for motorists, but narrow). Turn left in the main street to follow the road signposted to Buttermere. Return from Buttermere over Newlands Pass to Portinscale, back to Keswick. *30 miles.*

Tour 8. Borrowdale Road to Seatoller, over Honister Pass to Buttermere (the gradients on the pass are very steep, the first quarter of a mile down the Buttermere side of the pass being 1 in 3. Good brakes are essential, cyclists being advised to walk this section). Return either over Newlands Pass or continue along Crummock to Lorton, keep right on entering the village, over Whinlatter Pass to Braithwaite and Keswick. There is one sharp short rise on Whinlatter and a long descent into Braithwaite. (Coaches use this road regularly.) *26 miles via Whinlatter, 23 miles via Newlands.*

Tour 9. Braithwaite, Whinlatter Pass, Lorton; motorists turn left for Scale Hill and Loweswater, cyclists will find it better to continue over Lorton Bridge, then left through Thrackthwaite to Loweswater. Continue past the lake to Lamplugh, turn left after passing Lamplugh Arms, through Croasdale to visit Ennerdale Lake. Return to Lamplugh, and follow main roads to Cockermouth, Bassenthwaite and Keswick. *42 miles.*

Tour 10. Follow Tour 9 to Lamplugh then main road to Egremont, Calderbridge, Gosforth, keep left on entering Gosforth and again halfway through, and continue to keep left until the side of Wastwater is reached. Continue to Wasdale Head, visit the smallest church in the country. Return along the side of Wastwater, keeping left, to Santon Bridge and Eskdale. Return to Santon Bridge, Gosforth, Egremont, Cockermouth, Keswick. *97 miles.*

Tour 11. Penrith road to Troutbeck. Turn right, past the old station, over Matterdale Common to Ullswater. Visit Aira Force close

by the point where the road reaches the lake. Turn left along
Ullswater shore to Pooley Bridge, and on to Penrith (Penrith can be
avoided if desired by taking the left fork just before Pooley Bridge
and turning left at Stainton). Return by way of Penruddock to
Keswick. *39 miles (including Penrith).*

Tour 12. John Peel's Country. Carlisle road to Castle Inn, turn
right at the cross roads to Uldale, and over the moors to Caldbeck,
birthplace of John Peel, the famous Cumbrian huntsman, who spent
most of his life in this village and is buried in the churchyard. Keep
right at the village towards Penrith, turn right again at Hesket
Newmarket, through Mungrisedale, right again on reaching the main
road, back to Keswick. *36 miles.*

BORROWDALE

BORROWDALE IS FREQUENTLY CLASSED as part of Keswick, for
Keswick is the postal town for all the villages of that valley which
lies to the south of Derwentwater. It is roughly five miles long from
the Lake to Seathwaite and contains five small villages or hamlets.

The first is Grange with its charming twin bridge, a subject beloved
of artists. The valley now passes through the jaws of Borrowdale,
formed by Castle Crag and Grange Fell which tower on either side
of the valley. The main road keeps to the left and the river scenery
between Grange and Rosthwaite is probably the finest in the country,
a splendid contrast between its rugged shapely fells and its perfectly
level green strath. Seats are placed at vantage points overlooking the
river and the visitor is advised to allow ample time to appreciate it.
The Bowder Stone lies a short distance off the main road on the
left. On the opposite side of the river from Grange, a rough road
follows the course of the river, later to become a footpath which
follows the river right to Seatoller.

Half a mile beyond Rosthwaite the road which leads to
Stonethwaite, the start of the Langstrath Valley, strikes off to the left.
The main road sweeps round below Glaramara to Seatoller, which
lies at the foot of Honister Pass. At a signpost about one hundred
yards before Seatoller, a road branching to the left leads to
Seathwaite a mile beyond. Seathwaite, consisting of a farm and
cottages, lies in wild romantic country facing Sour Milk Ghyll, at the
foot of Sty Head Pass.

Keen walkers will find that any of the spots in Borrowdale make
good centres for the fells; in fact, for those who prefer the quiet of
the countryside to the noise of the towns, they are the finest centres
for fell climbing in the Lake District.

From Grange to Seatoller there is a secondary road to the right of the river which leads to the foot of Castle Crag, 900 feet, which is worth a short detour taking fifteen to twenty minutes, to climb to the summit, for the magnificent view of Borrowdale and Derwentwater. On the top is the site of an ancient British hill-fort. A grassy footpath from the foot of the Crag leads to Seatoller, a short and attractive walk.

AROUND BORROWDALE

Being a valley with steep fells on either side, Borrowdale has few walks of the easy class to offer, the few consist of walking along one side of the valley and returning along the other. The following four walks are of this class.

Route 21. From Grange, a rough road starts next to the café, which leads up the right-hand side of the river. About a mile along, where the road crosses a stream, you can either follow a riverside footpath which leads past Longthwaite Youth Hostel to Seatoller, four miles, or by the rough road which ascends to the foot of Castle Crag already mentioned, and then by a green footpath along the fell side to Seatoller. *3 miles.*

Route 22. Grange to Rosthwaite by the main road. This is one of very few main roads that can be recommended to the walker because of the beautiful scenery it embraces. The Bowder Stone can also be included by a diversion to the left, half a mile from Grange. Turn right down a lane at Rosthwaite, cross the river and return by the track on the other side to Grange, or in the opposite direction by a footpath to Seatoller. *4 miles.*

Route 23. Bus to Seatoller. Then follow the road which commences at a signpost a short distance from the village of Seatoller towards Keswick, and leads to Seathwaite. Where the road crosses the river, pass through a gate on the right and keep to the right of the river to the foot of Sour Milk Ghyll, a fine cascade. Cross the river by the Ramblers' Bridge to the farms at Seathwaite. This bridge was presented to the National Trust in 1945 as a token of Lake District ramblers' appreciation of the services of those who fought in the Second World War. Return by the road to Seatoller. *2½ miles.*
This walk can be extended if desired by continuing up the valley to Stockley Bridge. Here the track forks, one goes left up Grains Ghyll to Sprinkling Tarn and Esk Hause, the other, which is the one to follow, rises fairly sharply over rough ground for a short distance, after which is an easy walk past Sty Head Tarn to the top of Sty Head Pass. At this point there is a good view down the valley to

Wordsworth's Home   The Parlour

Grasmere   Swan Inn

Langdale

Dungeon Ghyll Old Hotel

Wasdale, immediately to the right is Great Gable and the fine crags of Great End appear in front to the left. Another mile of easy walking leads past Sprinkling Tarn to the top of Esk Hause where Esk Pike, Bowfell and the Langdale Pikes appear in view. Behind is a splendid view of Great Gable.

Return the same way to the wooden bridge below Sty Head Tarn, cross the bridge and follow the path down the left side of Sty Head Ghyll. Lower down is a close view of the very fine Taylor Ghyll Force. The path continues down the valley towards Seathwaite, which can be reached by crossing the Ramblers' Bridge, or you can keep to the same side of the river if returning direct to Seatoller.

You can also return down Grains Ghyll, which starts on the right-hand side of Sprinkling Tarn, to Stockley Bridge. It is the steepest but shortest route.

The great advantage of this walk is that one can return from any point desired. The full distance to the top of Esk Hause from Seatoller is 4 miles.

Route 24. By Borrowdale bus to Stonethwaite Road End—the first signposted road on the left after leaving Rosthwaite by the main road. The narrow road passes the church to the hamlet of Stonethwaite and continues up the valley for a three-quarter mile.

At this point the valley forks, the left rising up to Greenup whilst the right is the Langstrath Valley (the long valley). A short distance up here the river is crossed by a wooden footbridge and the track follows the valley for two miles to the foot of Stake Pass. Cross the river by a footbridge and return down the opposite side to Stonethwaite. *7 miles.*

Strenuous Fell Climbs

The following walks are all fairly strenuous fell climbs. Those who attempt these should be well shod and prepared for rough and sometimes boggy ground.

Route 25. BUTTERMERE. By Borrowdale bus to Seatoller. Then follow the main road up Honister Pass; at the top, turn left through the Slate Works and follow the route of an old dismantled railway up a steep incline to the ruined Drum House at the top. From here continue along the track ahead which leads down the side of Fleetwith Pike into Warnscale Bottom and Gatesgarth. Follow the main road past the farm until it leaves the lake shore, then along an interesting footpath by the shores of Buttermere (at one point the path is tunnelled right through the rock face) to the end of the lake; a waymarked footpath to the right leads to Buttermere village. The return may be made either by walking over Honister Pass or via Whinlatter. *Seatoller to Buttermere 7 miles.*

D

An interesting alternative, entailing a little extra climbing, is to turn sharp right at the Drum House, cross a small piece of flat land, then climb up the fell side in front; there is a footpath, but it is not easy to find at first. Bear slightly left and beware of the great precipices of Honister Crag which lie to the right. The path which skirts the top of the crags leads on to Fleetwith Pike, a magnificent view point with the three lakes, Buttermere, Crummock and Loweswater, in a line. The descent is made in a direct line towards Buttermere, taking care to keep to the path down the top of the ridge as there are crags on either side. The path finally leads to the Honister Pass road near Gatesgarth.

Route 26. GREAT GABLE. This is the finest and one of the most popular Lakeland peaks, only fifty-one feet below the 3,000 feet line. It is almost surrounded by magnificent crags and great care is required in climbing it. Strangers should not attempt it without a guide when the tops are cloud-capped. With care, it is perfectly safe in good weather.

Great Gable

There are several routes from Seatoller. One is to follow Route 25 as far as the Drum House, when a well-marked footpath strikes off to the left, goes under Grey Knotts, on to Brandreth. Another path starts from the Slate Works, climbing the fell side on to Grey Knotts, joining the other on Brandreth. The route continues along the tops

on to Green Gable, drops sharply to cross Windy Gap, then up a very
rough rocky track, easy to follow, to the summit of Great Gable.
Note the Fell and Rock Climbing Club Memorial Tablet on the side
of the cairn.

The view is very extensive, including four lakes, Crummock Water,
Windermere, Derwentwater and Wastwater. Many famous peaks can
be seen, the most prominent being the Scafell group across the
valley.

Another route from Seatoller is to proceed to Seathwaite and climb
by the path to the left of Sour Milk Ghyll, along Base Brown, where
the path rises to join the one from Brandreth to Green Gable.

A third route is to the top of Sty Head Pass as in Route 23, then
at the signpost at the top of the pass an easy footpath leads up
the fell side in a direct line for the summit. This route is one of the
best to follow in the descent of Great Gable, and a second return
route is by the rocky track on to Windy Gap, then by a path which
drops in a direct line for Sty Head Tarn, down Aaron's Slack, then
down Sty Head Pass by either side of the Ghyll to Seathwaite and
Seatoller.

There is a fourth route known as the Traverse, which passes Kearn
Knotts, Napes Needle and other famous rock climbs, but it is
dangerous and difficult to find and should only be attempted with an
experienced guide.

It is difficult to measure fell climbs in mileage, but the climbs
should take two to three hours from Seatoller.

Route 27. SCAFELL PIKE (3,120 feet). This is the highest
English peak and the tracks are easy to follow. There are two
routes from Seathwaite, one via Esk Hause, the other by the Guides
Route. For either continue along the path to Stockley Bridge;
here the track forks, the left hand runs along Grains Ghyll to
Sprinkling Tarn and then bears left to Esk Hause. After the first
half-mile it is a long and tedious climb and inclined to be wet
underfoot in places. The right-hand track, which passes Sty Head
Tarn and then bears left towards Sprinkling Tarn, although longer by
about half a mile, is the easier.

A short distance above Sprinkling Tarn a footpath begins on the
right and winds round the side of Great End, swings left again along
the top of the fell between Broad and Ill Crags. It becomes very
rocky in parts, but is easy to follow to the summit which should be
reached within three hours of leaving Seathwaite.

The alternative route is from the top of Sty Head Pass, reached
by the right-hand track from Stockley Bridge. Where the pony tracks
swing left towards Sprinkling Tarn another footpath, not easy to see
at first, starts a few yards from the signpost to the right and passes
under the crags of Great End. This is known as the Guides Route;

it continues at an easy gradient crossing Greta Ghyll and Piers Ghyll. After passing the latter it rises a short distance to a point not far from the top of Lingmell, which can be seen to the right. Take the left fork by a cairned route over rough rocky ground to the summit.

A good plan is to climb Scafell Pike by this route and return by Esk Hause and Sprinkling Tarn. The latter route is easy to follow from the top.

The view, which includes Windermere, Derwentwater and Wastwater, embraces many well-known peaks with Great Gable and Pillar prominent to the north. To the west, immediately below the summit, is a narrow ridge called Mickledore, easy to walk across, and at the far end is the sheer precipice of Scafell, which is about fifty feet lower than the Pike. If time and energy permit it is worth while continuing along Mickledore, then at the far end turn right immediately at the foot of the crag face. The path drops down a rough scree track to the bottom of a deep gully between two buttresses; this is called Lord's Rake. The route rises up this gully, over the top, rises and falls twice, and then left by a rough scree gully to the top of the fell. It takes about an hour from the Pike summit. A shorter route starts above the chock stone near the top of Lord's Rake, to the left up Deep Ghyll. A sharp screen scramble leads to the top of Scafell pinnacle, the best viewpoint. Erosion has made Lord's Rake dangerous.

It is a rough climb and on no account should it be attempted in bad weather. Its many fine crags make Scafell one of the most interesting fells to climb, but the view itself has no advantage over Scafell Pike.

The return should be made along the same route down Lord's Rake if returning to Borrowdale, and care should be taken on the climb to note where the descent commences off the top of the fell.

If possible, it is a better plan to start from the summit cairn in the direction of Wastwater and follow a path which leads down a long grassy slope to Burnmoor, the small tarn on the moors to the left of Wastwater. From the tarn you can either turn right along the track to Wasdale Head, or left to Eskdale where the night could be spent. It is also possible to descend either by Fox's Tarn and Cam Spout, or Slight Side to Eskdale.

Route 28. GLARAMARA. This is the huge mass at the head of Borrowdale, with Langstrath Valley on one side and the Seathwaite Valley on the other. Climbed by the following route, it makes a most interesting round with little hard climbing, the Sty Head Pass above Stockley Bridge being the most difficult.

Follow the previous route to the top of Esk Hause. On the immediate left as you arrive is a peak with a cairn on the top. Ten to twenty minutes' easy climbing leads to this cairn on the summit of Allen Crags, 150 feet above Esk Hause. The view includes Bowfell, Crinkle Crags, Scafell, Langdale Pikes, Windermere, Fairfield and the Helvellyn range. Close at hand is Great Gable.

Leave the summit in the direction of Great Gable; slightly right, a footpath travels along the fell, passing several pools named Lingcomb Tarns. Later the path drops slightly, bears to the right of some crags and rises round the top to a cairn overlooking the Grain Ghyll. Next it crosses over to more cairns on the north-east marking the summit of Glaramara which gives a grand view of Derwentwater and the surrounding fells.

A short distance below the summit cairn towards the south a slender pointed cairn on the left marks the start of a track which descends by way of Thornthwaite Fell down to the level of Comb Ghyll, and soon after the main road is joined near Seatoller. *9 miles. (Moderate.)*

Route 29. BOWFELL. Follow Route 24 to the foot of Stake Pass, half an hour's easy climbing leads to the summit marked by a cairn. Turn sharp right along a path which winds round some boggy land, then cuts across a narrow band called Gavel Moor for a mile and a quarter. At the far end it is rather boggy and it is advisable to keep as far left as possible until the pony track up Rossett Ghyll is reached near to Angle Tarn.

Pass round the foot of the tarn, and about twenty yards up the pass strike off to the left up the grassy slope to a gap between the two fells in front. At the top of Ewer Gap a good footpath crosses from Esk Pike; turn left and follow this for about half an hour until the top of Bowfell is reached. The last few yards are very rocky, but the view from the top is superb.

Return by the same path to Ewer Gap and continue up the next rise on to Esk Pike, and then down to Esk Hause. Avoid mistaking the path which rises to the left to Scafell Pike: the path from Esk Hause *drops* to Sprinkling Tarn, then you can return either by Grain Ghyll or Sty Head Pass to Seathwaite. *13½ miles. (Strenuous.)*

Route 30. LANGDALE PIKES. Follow the previous route to the summit of Stake Pass. A path to the left of the pony track rises between the two heights of Thunacar and Pike o' Stickle; the latter is worth a slight detour to climb, there is a fine view of Gimmer Crag to the south. Beyond these two heights the path rises sharply to the left of some crags to the summit of Harrison Stickle.

Pike o' Stickle and Harrison Stickle form the famous Langdale Pikes. The Langdale Valley lies deep below the foot of Harrison Stickle and away down the valley can be seen Windermere Lake. The mountain aspect is also very good, but cannot equal that to be seen later from High Raise.

Return from the summit a short distance along the same path and keep in a northerly direction along a well-marked footpath which rises up to Thunacar Knott and on to High Raise (or High White Stones). This point is frequently considered to be the centre of the Lake District, and the wonderful view of the fells in every direction gives the visitor this impression. Almost every high peak in the district can be seen, Great Gable being the most prominent to the west. In the distance are the Scottish fells to the west and Yorkshire fells to the east, with Morecambe Bay and Lancashire fells to the south.

Continue north by a wire fence which drops to Greenup where four footpaths meet, take the left one down Greenup Ghyll, crossing the second bridge over the river in the bottom and continue on to Stonethwaite. *12 miles. (Fairly strenuous.)*

Route 31. DALE HEAD. From Seatoller take the road to the top of Honister Pass. Turn right opposite the slate quarries by a path rising sharply to the left of a wire fence which forms a good guide to the summit of Dale Head. A walk over the tops on to Robinson is described in Route 19. To return to Borrowdale go to the right down the steep side of Dale Head to the small tarn in the bottom. The track rises slightly on to Lobstone Band, then descends to the right down the fell side by the quarries into Rosthwaite. *5 miles. (Fairly strenuous.)*

Route 32. FAR EASEDALE, GRASMERE. By Borrowdale bus to Rosthwaite. From Rosthwaite start up the valley to Stonethwaite, cross the river by a bridge opposite the houses, and then proceed up the valley with the river on the right. Soon the Langstrath Valley forks off to the right while our path rises to the left up Greenup Ghyll to the top of Greenup. After dropping sharply it continues as a pleasant walk down the long valley of Far Easedale: keep the beck on your left as you drop down the slope. At the bottom the widening river is crossed by a footbridge. Soon a road appears which leads down to Grasmere. Bus to Keswick and Borrowdale. *8 miles from Stonethwaite to Grasmere. (Fairly strenuous.)*

Route 33. THE FOUR PASSES. This is a popular round covering the four passes. Starting from Seatoller, proceed through Seathwaite to the top of Sty Head Pass and down the far side to Wasdale Head. A short distance before reaching the Wastwater Hotel a pony track starts on the right, a stone wall separating the track from Mosedale Beck on the left. The track continues up Mosedale, crosses Gatherstone Beck and rises round the side of Kirk Fell over Black Sail Pass, descending on the other side to the head of the Ennerdale Valley; note the glacier moraines, small hillocks on the opposite side of the valley. Passing the Youth Hostel, a track, Scarth Gap Pass, starts on the right leading over the Gap into the head of Buttermere. Join the main road at Gatesgarth, and follow this over Honister Pass to Seatoller. *21 miles. (Strenuous.)*

Route 34. ENNERDALE. Seatoller, up Honister Pass, to the Drum House (see Route 25), then take the path to the left which goes along the fell side below Grey Knotts and Brandreth. Instead of rising to the left on to the latter continue down to the right of a small beck, Tongue Beck, into the head of the Ennerdale Valley. Follow the road down the Liza Valley and along the shore of Ennerdale Lake; after a while the road leaves the lake, up a hill, passes through a gate, then immediately a track strikes off to the left leading back to shore of the lake again.

A pleasant diversion starts where the road leaves the lake, by following a footpath which hugs the shore, passing some picnic tables, round the end of Bowness Point (a diversion to the old look-out post on the top is worthwhile for the view of the lake), joining the bridle road further along: this follows the lake-shore for about two miles, to the water works at the foot of the lake. Cross the river by a footbridge, and turn right through a gate and follow a rough road to the pump house, bear right past here, and follow a road which gradually improves for the next mile to Ennerdale Bridge where an infrequent bus may be caught to Whitehaven on certain days of the week. For latest information consult Cumberland Motor Services Ltd., Whitehaven. On other days it will be necessary to walk by the road to Rowrah, three miles, or Wath Brow, three and a half miles, where there is a frequent bus service to Whitehaven, and an hourly service from there to Keswick. *Distance to Ennerdale Bridge from Seatoller, 13 miles. (Moderate.)*

Route 35. ESKDALE. To enjoy this tour it is advisable to spend one night in Eskdale, visiting Stanley Ghyll during that stay.

Follow Route 23 to the top of Esk Hause. A footpath starts from the shelter, a stone wall built in the shape of a cross, and begins to drop between the two paths which rise towards Scafell Pike and Esk Pike until it reaches Cam Spout, a noted waterfall.

There is now a choice of two routes, both attractive. The right-hand path continues under Slight Side and winds along the fell bottom for some two miles before zigzagging down the fell side to the left of Cowcove Beck to the valley, crossing the beck in the bottom by a bridge which gives a good view of the Cowcove Falls. The track continues past Taw House, and joins the road just beyond Wha House Bridge. The Youth Hostel is a short distance down the road, with an hotel next door, and several more at Boot, a mile beyond.

The left-hand path from Cam Spout keeps to the left of the beck and follows its course down to an interesting pack-horse bridge below Lingcove double falls, with Esk Falls below it. Across the bridge the path travels down the Esk Valley, to Brotherilkeld at the foot of Hard Knott Pass, where it joins the road which leads down the valley to Boot.

Boot can be avoided and a mile saved by following a signposted footpath which starts to the left of Woolpack Inn, and follows a track marked with white crosses by Eel Tarn over Burnmoor to Burnmoor Tarn.

At Boot cross the bridge and turn through a gate on the right. A pony track rises up to Burnmoor, passing the Burnmoor Tarn, and later drops into Wasdale, passing round the head of the lake.

Crossing the river by a concrete bridge, the track passes through a gate on to the main road. Turn right along here to Wasdale Head.

The shortest route to Seatoller from here is by Sty Head Pass, which takes about two hours for an average walker. *The distance between Seatoller and Boot by either route is about 13 miles.*

WINDERMERE and BOWNESS-on-WINDERMERE

Population: 8,540
Early Closing Day: Thursday
Tourist Information Centre: Victoria Street
National Park Centre The Glebe, Bowness-on-Windermere, and (summer only): Brockhole

WINDERMERE VILLAGE STANDS ABOUT 2 MILES from the lake from which it takes its name. Here is the railway station which is the terminus of the line. The houses of the little place extend southwards until they link up with Bowness, a little more than a mile and a half to the south.

Windermere has the advantage of small, easily reached eminences from which most comprehensive and panoramic views can be obtained. Probably the finest of these is Orrest Head, which is reached by entering the second of two gates immediately below Windermere Hotel, near the station, and following the zigzag path through the woods to the top. Immediately below is Windermere village, while the lake spreads out before you. Opposite Bowness Bay are the pretty islands which appear almost to cut the lake in two; behind the far shore rises the well-wooded heights of Claife, presenting in the spring a charming picture of innumerable shades of green foliage, in the summer a somewhat more uniform tint of yellow-green and later a magnificent spectacle of rich autumnal colouring—yellow and

Grasmere
TO KESWICK
TO PENRITH
B5343
Grasmere
A591
Rydal
Rydal Water
Chapel Stile
Ambleside
Skelwith Bridge
Waterhead
Troutbeck
Furness Fells
Troutbeck Bridge
A593
B5285
TO KENDAL
Hawkshead
WINDERMERE
Coniston
Claife Heights
Bowness-on-Windermere
Esthwaite Water
B5285
B5284
Coniston Water
Far Sawrey
TO BROUGHTON IN FURNESS
Grisedale
Winster
Forest
Gill Head
A5074
Satterthwaite
0   1   2
Scale of Miles
Lake Side
A592
TO ULVERSTON
Newby Bridge

Crown Copyright Reserved
GEOGRAPHIA LTD.

red, brown and gold, with here and there dense masses of dark green Scotch fir amidst the oak, beech, larch and birch which predominate.

There is also a wonderful view of the amphitheatre of fells which surround Windermere, and a chart on the top indicates the various points in view.

Queen Adelaide's Hill

Other grand view points near Windermere are Biskey Howe and Queen Adelaide's Hill; the former is reached in a few minutes from the Lake Road by various footpaths and gives a grand view of the southern half of the lake. Queen Adelaide's Hill, now National Trust property, is reached from Bowness by the Rayrigg Road, and from Windermere by the new Birthwaite Road. Seats are placed along the route for enjoying the exquisite views of the lake and fells.

BOWNESS

Bowness stands alongside the lake, and lying as it does much lower down than Windermere village it does not command such distant views, but it has the advantage of looking across the lake upon scenes of the richest beauty. Bowness Bay is one of the prettiest spots in the Lake District, a beautiful promenade extends along the lake shore, delightfully shaded with beech trees and furnished with seats from which the fine panorama of lake and fells can be enjoyed. Unfortunately, it has become rather commercialised and is frequently crowded during summer weekends.

Bowness church, close to the lake and surrounded by yew trees, is an interesting building. It was built in the sixteenth century on the site of a much earlier edifice. Notice the fine east window with its stained-glass pictures; the glass was brought here from Cartmel Priory when it was dissolved in 1537.

LAKE WINDERMERE

Windermere is the largest of the English lakes, being ten and half miles long and one and a quarter miles wide in its broadest part. It extends from Waterhead at the head of the lake down to Lake Side at the foot. At Lake Side there is a privately-owned steam railway which runs to Haverthwaite; across the platform is the boating berth. A service of Ribble buses connects Lake Side with Ulverston. During the summer British Rails' fleet of yachts, which includes two modern motor yachts, sail several times a day along the lake between Lake Side and Waterhead, calling at Bowness. A sail up the lake is a trip of delight and beauty.

Proceeding up the lake we pass Blake Holme on the eastern shore,

and a panorama of fells opens out in front; the Kentmere and
Fairfield groups, and the fine cluster at the head of the lake. On the
eastern shore is Storr's Hall Hotel, and then after passing Ramp
Holme the Ferry Hotel pier is observed on the left. A ferry for
pedestrians, cycles, cars and small coaches crosses the lake at
frequent intervals between here and the opposite shore.

The islands which lie opposite Bowness Bay are now reached; the
largest is Belle Isle, named after Miss Isabella Curwen for whom the
island was purchased in 1781; she was heiress to vast Cumberland
wealth and the last representative of a family who had been settled
at Workington for six and a half centuries. She married her cousin,
John Christian, or Ewanrigg, who became Member of Parliament
for Carlisle and then for Cumberland, and they made their home on
this island which remains in the family's possession and is open
to visitors, Sundays to Thursdays, from Spring Bank Holiday until
the end of September.

Threading its way between the islands, the boat arrives in
Bowness Bay, where passengers may alight at the pier.

Wray Castle

Leaving Bowness pier, the boat continues up the lake past the
island of Lady Holme where for centuries stood a chapel dedicated
to St. Mary the Virgin. All remains of it have long since disappeared.
The lake shore is well wooded and extremely attractive. On the left,
opposite Low Wood Hotel pier, is Wray Castle, a castellated building
of modern structure commanding beautiful views; it is now National
Trust property and was the first and, for some time, only Lakeland
Youth Hostel. As the boat approaches the head of the lake, the lofty
fells beyond Ambleside come into view, disposed with rare grandeur
of outline and magnificence of colour. Along the western shore, as
far as High Wray, a range of rocky fells rises over the water, covered
here and there with birch, oak, hazel and pine, and patches of
bracken bright green in summer, copper colour in the autumn, and
the purple and black heather.

Passengers land at the head of the lake at Waterhead pier, which
is a mile from the town of Ambleside. There is a pleasant bay and
promenade to the left of the pier as you leave it, from which rowing-
boats and motor launches ply for hire.

The buses stop near the pier entrance for Ambleside. But the walk
is pleasant if the lower road and footpath through the fields is taken.
The village is only ten to fifteen minutes' walk from the pier.

Sir Henry Seagrave

Windermere (like Coniston) was the scene of many attempts on
the world water speed record. However, they ceased on Windermere
when Sir Henry Seagrave was killed on the lake on 13th June, 1930.

AROUND WINDERMERE

Route 36. WINSTER. Start from Windermere station by the main road up the hill towards Kendal. At the first farm turn right down a footpath crossing the railway to Droomer Farm. A lane winds along the slopes of School Knott for a half-mile, then a path is followed in an easterly direction to Hag End and Borwick Fold.

From here a long lane leads in the direction of Crook; turn right at the crossroads at Beckside to join the main road close by the church, which is worth visiting. Pass down a lane to the left of the church to Gilpin Mill, turn right to Knipe Tarn, and on to Winster.

Proceed a short distance down the road towards the lake, then at High Hill fork right and follow the lane passing to the right of Lindeth Tarn, across the main road and along Brant Fell, turning either left at the farm by the lane to Bowness or along one of several footpaths to Windermere. *14 miles. (Moderate.)*

Route 37. ESTHWAITE WATER. Cross the lake by the ferry to Ferry Hotel and follow the road to Near Sawrey. On the left is 'Hill Top' where Beatrix Potter wrote the *Peter Rabbit* books. It was bequeathed to the National Trust and is open to the public. Then take the road on either side of Esthwaite Water to Hawkshead. It is a quaint, picturesque old village with the Grammar School where William Wordsworth, the Lakeland poet, was educated from 1778 to 1783; within the school is a desk on which the poet carved his initials. The church, which overlooks the village, is worth a visit, the most interesting feature being the altar tomb with effigies of William and Mary Sandys, 1578. There is also a curious old muniment chest.

Continue along the road towards Coniston, forking right at Hawkshead Hall. The Hall was erected at the time of Henry III and belonged to the monks of Furness Abbey. The Court House was added in the fourteenth century and is now in the care of the National Trust. It is a Folk Museum of rural crafts.

A short distance along the road fork right again up a lane and take the second lane on the right to Crag. A footpath starts on the left and crosses the heights to Belle Grange on the shores of Windermere. Follow the shore road down the lake back to the Ferry Hotel for the ferry. *10 miles. (Fairly easy.)*

Part of the footpath through the forestry on Claife Heights is a marked Nature Walk, and instructions for following this can be obtained from the National Parks Centre at Brockhole or County Hall, Kendal.

Route 38. TARN HOWS. Follow Route 37 to Hawkshead. Proceed up the lane opposite the Red Lion, passing under an arch. Just beyond is the house where Wordsworth lodged. A short distance up the hill a signpost on the right directs the walker through two fields to The Tarns. Fine views are obtained of Helvellyn, Ill Bell, Harter Fell and the Coniston group. The path leads to a road, a short distance along which a lane signposted to The Tarns forks off to the right beside a Baptist chapel. This lane crosses the Ambleside–Coniston road then rises between two stone walls. At the top of the hill is a signpost on the right pointing through a gate to the viewpoint. All of Coniston may be seen and a wonderful panorama of fells all round extending as far as Saddleback in the north.

A few hundred yards farther, one of the prettiest lakes in the district comes into view, Highlow Tarn, commonly called Tarn Hows. Turn left and by the shore until you reach the dam at the foot of the lake and follow the stream down Glen Mary to the road below. Turn left along the road for about three-quarters of a mile to a road signposted to Tilberthwaite.

A footpath starts on the right through a wood, joining the main road again near to Coniston. *11 miles (Moderate.)* Another signposted footpath, also leading to Coniston village, starts opposite Yew Tree Farm.

Route 39. INGS. Almost opposite Windermere railway station, near the bus stop, a signposted footpath leads to the top of Orrest Head. From a point towards the top of the Head a path strikes off to the left leading to Causey Farm; turn right to follow the lane to Ings. Look round the church, then take the lane over the River Gowan to Ings Hall. After going under the railway turn right to Hag End and cross the common to a lane on the right past Droomer Farm to Windermere Station. *7 miles. (Fairly easy.)*

Route 40. NEWBY BRIDGE. The walk requires little description, it is simply to follow the main road by the lake to Newby Bridge and return by the road along the opposite shore to the Ferry Hotel. About a mile before reaching Newby Bridge is Fell Foot, a small country park opened by the National Trust in 1972. Here there is a large car park, a café, and several chalets which can be rented. Distance from Bowness to Newby Bridge is eight miles, and part or all of this can be covered by bus. The walk back by Lake Side and Low Graythwaite is through charming scenery. *7 miles. (Easy.)*

Route 41. WRAY. By bus to Ferry Road End. This is a similar walk to Route 40 but by the upper reaches of the lake. Cross the ferry and follow the shore route to Wray. You can continue on foot to Ambleside by joining the main road.

Alternatively there is a very pleasant walk from Little Sawrey to Wise Een Tarn and over Claiffe Heights, right from the tarn to Wray Castle, then by boat to Waterhead. *6 miles. (Easy.)*

Route 42. GRISEDALE AND CONISTON. By bus to Ferry
Nab, and by ferry across the lake. Follow the road to Near Sawrey,
the second village; on the left is 'Hill Top', home of the late Beatrix
Potter. Turn left along the road signposted to Lake Side, then keep
right, crossing the river near Esthwaite Water. Take the second road
on the left for a few yards, then up a wide track on the right which
leads over the fells down into the next valley at Grisedale Hall,
which housed prominent German prisoners during the Second World
War and was demolished in 1958.

Opposite the main entrance to the Hall, go down a lane, through
a gate, and a short distance beyond take the right-hand track which
rises obliquely alongside a wall. It rises gradually for a mile and a
half.

All this area is heavily planted, and it is necessary to follow the
signs through the forest by a forest road which joins the main road
at Brantwood. Follow the road around the head of the lake to
Coniston village.

Bus from Waterhead Hotel or Crown Hotel (village) to Ambleside.
Ferry to Coniston. *11 miles. (Moderate.)*

There is a Nature Trail and observation posts in Grisedale Forest.
Write for particulars to the Forestry Commission, Grisedale Hall,
Satterthwaite, Lancs.

AMBLESIDE

Population: 3,000
Early Closing Day: Thursday
Market Day: Wednesday
Tourist Information Centre: The Old Court House
National Trust: Broadlands, Borrans Road
National Park Centre: The Old Court House, Church Street.
Information Caravan Waterhead Car Park.

AMBLESIDE IS THE PRINCIPAL CENTRE for the southern part of
the Lake District, and is second only to Keswick as the best centre
for all the area. Most places, excepting the western lakes, can be
reached with ease in a day's excursion from Ambleside; the quickest
approach to the west for the walker or cyclist is by Wrynose and
Hard Knott passes. Ambleside is easily accessible from all parts of
the country, the express Ribble buses from Lancashire and Yorkshire
to Keswick all stop at Ambleside. There is a good local service
between Windermere railway station and Ambleside, or it can be
reached by sailing up the lake from Lake Side or Bowness.

Within a short distance there are many delightful walks and

some charming country. The town is bounded on the north by
Nab Scar, Fairfield and High Pike; on the east by Red Screes and
Wansfell; on the west by Loughrigg, all fells over the 1,000 feet
contour. Ambleside is drained by the River Rothay and its tributaries,
the Scandale and the Stock. It is situated on the main road through
the Lakes to Keswick, and also near the start of Kirkstone Pass and
the Langdale Valley.

It is pre-eminently a clean and healthy place, and has many
excellent hotels and boarding houses for holiday makers. Its shops
are up to date and well equipped, and its water, taken from the
Scandale Beck, has been declared by authorities to be almost the
purest in England.

In 1650 a charter for a market was granted to Ambleside. In
1688 James II granted a similar charter and power to collect tolls
for the benefit of the poor. The market rights are now vested in
the Ambleside Charity Trust, and the income assists to provide the
services of a nurse for the district. Fairs are now held in Whit-week
and October, when Herdwick sheep exchange hands.

Another link with the past is the quaintly picturesque Rushbearing
festival held the last weekend in July. The origin of the floral
procession, church service and field day is said to be a mixture of
the ancient Roman floralia, the old English custom of strewing the
church floor with rushes before tiled floors came into vogue, and a
thanksgiving and merrymaking after the hay was safely gathered in.
The Rushbearing hymn, composed over eighty years ago by Owen
Lloyd, a friend of Hartley Coleridge, is sung annually in the Market
Place. The event has been immortalized by Wordsworth.

One of the attractions of Ambleside is the museum, which contains
Roman articles which were recovered between 1913 and 1920 from
the site of the Roman fort in Borrans Field at the head of Lake
Windermere. The field belongs to the National Trust and is open
free to the public. The site was excavated under the superintendence
of Mr. R. G. Collingwood, to whom the arrangements of the exhibits
and models of the two forts in the museum are wholly due.

Another point of interest is the Church of St. Mary. It was built
in 1854 when the old church became too small to accommodate
visitors. It is of dark grey stone and was designed by Sir Gilbert
Scott, who was amongst the first to discover its incongruity; it would
look much better in a city street. It possesses a costly and handsome
reredos, and there are memorial windows to the late Rt. Hon. W. E.
Forster, who was Irish Secretary in 1880, and to William Wordsworth.
The latter is in the Wordsworth memorial chapel, dedicated in 1952.
The furnishings include two oak chairs which belonged to the poet.
In the west end of the churchyard there is a handsome column with a
touching inscription to Forster. The peal of eight bells is classed
among the best in the north, but they are not rung at present.

On the Keswick road a short distance from the village is a small house built on a bridge, the Old Bridge House. It is now a National Trust Enquiry and Information Office.

Guided walks for visitors led by Voluntary Wardens start from Waterhead car park during summer weekends. Details from the Information Caravan in the car park.

AROUND AMBLESIDE

Route 43. STOCK GHYLL FORCE. This attractive waterfall is one of the popular features of Ambleside, it is an easy climb from the town, starting by the Salutation Hotel.

Go through the park gates—notice the old bobbin mill and its mill dam—and proceed along the banks of the beck. The roar of water announces our approach to the falls, and suddenly there bursts into view through the trees a foaming cascade, leaping over a huge V-shaped boulder down 76 feet to the rocks below. There is a wonderful show of daffodils in the spring.

Route 44. JENKYN'S CRAG. This is a delightful and popular walk through the woods making a pleasant stroll of one to two hours. From the town, follow the main road towards Waterhead, cross the car park about half a mile from town on the left, join a narrow road on the far side, and up the hill to the right. Follow the signposted track towards Jenkyn's Crag. On entering a wood, fork left at a signpost marked 'To Waterhead', climb to the left of the beck, cross the bridge higher up, then by a short cut on the right to join the track higher up. Soon after, a signpost, on the left, to Kelsick Scar, is passed; a few yards beyond cross a stile on the right which brings you on to Jenkyn's Crag above Waterhead. The fell aspect is very fine, but much of the lake is hidden by the trees. The most prominent fells are the Langdale Pikes, Crinkle Crags and Bowfell, Weatherham and Coniston Old Man, and much nearer at the head of the lake is Loughrigg.

An extra diversion can be included by returning to the signpost marked Kelsick Scar and ascending the track for a short distance. At the top on the left is a clearing which gives a good view of Bowfell and Scafell groups, but again much of the lower view is obstructed by the trees. The path continues with the lake on your right, then, after a quarter-mile, drops to join the Jenkyn's Crag track again. By turning left you can follow the track to Skelghyll and the Troutbeck road, or turn right and the track leads back to Ambleside by the same route as you came.

A path can be followed from Waterhead signpost which drops sharply, crosses an open field to a stile on the far side, then down a **very narrow lane to** join the main road immediately opposite the Waterhead Hotel. Bus to Ambleside. *2½ miles (not including Kelsick Scar, ½ mile). (Easy.)*

Route 45. STOCK GHYLL AND KIRKSTONE. Follow the road signposted to Stock Ghyll Force. It starts from the Salutation Hotel, or by footpath from Old Lake Road. Continue past the entrance to the falls and to the former Kelsick Grammar School, now part of the Charlotte Mason College, and follow the road to Middle Grove Farm. The road is metalled as far as the school gates and afterwards is quite a good road, but after passing the farm it becomes a rough fell road, and farther on, past an old ruined building, it becomes a mere footpath. Shortly after, the path veers to the left and drops towards the Kirkstone road which can be seen across the valley. Crossing a beck, it joins the road beside a ruined stone building. Kirkstone Inn at the head of Kirkstone Pass is about another half-mile up the road, and is worth visiting for the view of Brotherswater down the pass. Return down the road to Ambleside. *6 miles. (Easy.)*

Route 46. LOUGHRIGG. Follow the track by St. Mary's Church through the park, cross the River Rothay by the bridge, turn up the road opposite, pass through first gate, then over iron stile: soon there is a sign 'to Clappersgate'. Follow the path to next stile and where it points 'to the Lily Pond', proceed up the hill, cross a small beck and continue to the first cairned peak, 'Todd's Crag', from where there are extensive views. The highest point is a few yards further on: follow the path which descends to the right to a small pond, up the next rise and down to a small tarn. Pass to the right of this. Take the right hand track to a stone wall, keeping to the left of the wall to a gate and a major track. Several paths now lead to various parts of the fell.

To return to Ambleside, pass through the gate and follow the track down the hill: there is a footpath-sign lower down by a wall. The path descends to the farm where the road was left on the way out. Follow the road downhill, back to Ambleside. *2 miles. (Moderate.)*

Route 47. WANSFELL. Follow Route 46 past the Stock Ghyll Force and former Kelsick Grammar School entrances as far as the first gate across the road. A few yards beyond the gate an iron stile on the right marks the start of a footpath which leads up Wansfell. The climb is fairly steep but the ground is easy, although boggy in places. The path is easy to follow to the summit and the view from the top is one of the best around Windermere. As well as most of Lake Windermere being in sight there is a grand fell aspect, the

E

High Street range being particularly prominent. Other fells include
Black Combe, the Coniston fells, Scafell, Bowfell and part of
Dalehead.

Return to the gateway on the summit ridge, then take a path
roughly in the direction of Wray Castle which can be seen on the far
side of Windermere, dropping to High Skelghyll farm where a good
farm track is reached. Turn right and follow this back to Ambleside.
6 miles. (Fairly strenuous.)

Route 48. AROUND LOUGHRIGG. Follow the road by St.
Mary's Church and the park to cross the bridge over the River
Rothay. Turn right and follow the road for one and half miles to
Pelter Bridge. Do not cross the bridge, but continue along the track
on the left which passes along the southern shore of Rydal Water
and the foot of Grasmere to join the road on Red Bank. Keep to
the left along this road for half a mile then turn left up a lane to pass
Loughrigg Tarn on your right. Just beyond the tarn it bears to the
right and rejoins the road at Tarn Foot; cross the road and follow a
narrow lane to Skelwith Bridge. Bus to Ambleside. *Distance to
Skelwith Bridge 6 miles. (Easy.)*

Route 49. ELTERWATER. By bus to Skelwith Bridge. A
track starts immediately on the right of the bridge looking upstream,
passes some houses and a sawmill, then along a narrow foot-track
to Skelwith Force, about five minutes' walk. As a certain amount
of water is used to drive the sawmill, the falls are best seen when
the mill is not working, but at all times the surroundings are very
picturesque. A better view of the falls is obtained from the other
side of the river.

From Skelwith Bridge, follow the Coniston road for a few yards
then turn right along a track signposted 'To Skelwith Force'. After
passing the houses, follow a footpath on the right which leads to
the falls. Return to the main road and a few yards to the right is a
footpath signposted 'To Colwith Force'. Follow this for about
half a mile to a farm. Keep right at the last out-building and avoid
the road; the path goes through another field, down a very narrow
footlane, crosses a road, through more fields down to the river.
Shortly after, it crosses a stile on to the road. Turn right up the road
to the houses at Colwith.

Colwith Force may be visited at this point, it is on private ground
a short distance along the road to Wrynose on the left. The key
may be obtained at the house on the corner and the entrance is by a
wooden gate on the left a short distance up the road. There are
wooden steps down to the stream below the falls. Although the
setting is quite charming, the falls themselves are rather disappointing,
especially as seen from the right bank below.

Continue the walk from the foot of the hill and follow the road
to Elterwater. Although a main tarmac road, it passes through some
delightful scenery, wild raspberries growing profusely on the roadside
in July.

Soon the pleasant village of Elterwater is reached. The road crosses
the river, and on the far side a foot-track commences on the right.
This passes through a field and enters a thick wood by the shores of
Elterwater. Much of the lake is screened by trees until you reach the
far end. If returning direct to Skelwith Bridge, keep along this track.

Route 50. RETURN OVER LOUGHRIGG. To extend the walk,
leave the main track opposite a boathouse in the wood, and a
footpath rises to join the main road. Turn left to the first road on the
right, go up here to join another road coming from Elterwater towards
Grasmere. Turn right, then left at the next road junction.

Passing the houses at Scroggs, the wall on the right ends and a
footpath starts. Follow this path which rises diagonally in the direction
of the road for a short distance then, bearing right, rises up the hillside
until a magnificent view of Grasmere comes into sight.

The cairn marking the summit of the first peak can be seen to the
right, and this is the next objective. There is a good track coming
up direct from Grasmere almost in a line from the summit. On
arrival at this cairn, it will be seen that this is not the actual summit
of Loughrigg, but that there are several such peaks. Each peak is
worth visiting in turn for the different views obtained. Looking
over Grasmere from the first cairn is almost like looking down from
the gallery of a theatre. Ten minutes' walk to the second cairn to
the right brings into view Windermere and Esthwaite Water. Five
minutes to the next cairn gives a view of Loughrigg Tarn and the
Brathay Valley, and from the next cairn is a good view of Rydal
Water.

Loughrigg is a big elevation, 1,101 feet in the highest point, which
stretches from Grasmere to Windermere: it is about three miles long
and two miles wide. There are several well-marked tracks running
along it and it would be difficult to indicate any particular one. The
best suggestion is to keep heading for Windermere and whichever
track you take in that direction will eventually bring you out in the
right place. Nearer to the Windermere end, Ambleside comes into
view and this is your objective.

The great advantage of this walk is that it can be shortened at
several points by taking the bus back to Ambleside; buses run from
Skelwith Bridge, Elterwater, and Grasmere. For the latter, instead
of climbing Loughrigg, continue along the road towards Grasmere,
fork right at the first road junction by Loughrigg Terrace, then follow
a path on the left which drops to the river between Grasmere and
Rydal and crosses it by a wooden footbridge. A track leads up to

the road where buses run to Ambleside. *Skelwith Bridge to Colwith 1½ miles, Elterwater 3, to main road between Grasmere and Rydal 6½, by Loughrigg Fell to Ambleside 9. (Fairly easy.)*

For an easy walk, take bus to Grasmere and return over Loughrigg Fell to Ambleside. *4 miles from the footbridge.*

Route 51. BLEA TARN. Take the Coniston bus to Colwith road end. Walk down the road signposted 'Colwith Bridge'. Crossing the bridge, turn up the road to the left and follow this for one and a half miles, passing Little Langdale Tarn on your left. Immediately after passing a cattle grid across the road take the road to the right and about a mile along here is Blea Tarn on your left. It is seen to its best advantage by dropping to the tarn near its outlet; this is a favourite spot for artists and photographers for the famous view of Blea Tarn with the Langdale Pikes in the background.

Continue along the road, which winds down to the head of the Langdale Valley, fork right at Wall End Farm and join the valley road at the Old Dungeon Ghyll Hotel. Half a mile down the road to the right is the New Hotel, behind which are the famous Dungeon Ghyll Falls.

To reach the falls, go through two gates beyond the hotel stables and, leaving the side of Mill Ghyll, take the path to the left that crosses a field and goes through a gate in the wall. Turn right alongside the wall which will bring you to the falls.

The path leading up to the falls from the hotel can be followed to the top of Harrison Stickle, and the view from the top is very fine; it is a long steep climb, and is much better as a route for the descent. Return to Ambleside by bus from Dungeon Ghyll. *Walking distance 6 miles. (Easy.)*

Route 52. HARRISON STICKLE (one of the Langdale Pikes). By Ribble bus to Dungeon Ghyll. (Very infrequent service.) Alight at the New Dungeon Hotel and start along a footpath to the left of it: this rises sharply after crossing Mill Ghyll, and keeps close to the right side of the beck to its source at Stickle Tarn. The chief features of this tarn are the fine precipices of Pavey Ark which tower above on the far side.

The path forks just beyond the tarn, the left path which leads to Harrison Stickle rises sharply by the side of a beck and winds round to the left to the top of the crags of Pavey Ark. It goes along the top and finally rises to the summit of Harrison Stickle. Another rough and slightly dangerous track known as Jack's Rake rises diagonally up the crags themselves. It is shorter than going round.

The view to the south is very fine. Almost underneath is the Dungeon Ghyll Hotel, and across the valley the road winding up to Blea Tarn. Down the full length of the Langdale Valley appears

Windermere Lake at the bottom; Esthwaite Water and Elterwater
appear farther to the right. Of the fell aspect, Skiddaw and Saddleback appear to the north, farther to the left is Dalehead, Grisedale and
Grasmoor. Nearer at hand are Glaramara, Pillar, Scafell, Great Gable,
Bowfell, Crinkle Crags and, across Wrynose, the Coniston Fells. To
the east is the Helvellyn range and, beyond, the High Street range.

The descent requires care because of the many crags which abound
beneath the summit, and are difficult to see. Start along the path
which goes in a north-westerly direction towards Glaramara for about
one hundred yards, then turn left down to the beck below, over the
next rise, bearing left, to follow a rough and steep track which winds
down below Loft Crag to the New Dungeon Ghyll Hotel. Return
to Ambleside by bus. *Walking distance 6 miles. (Strenuous.)*

Route 53. SCANDALE. Starting from the Old Bridge House go
along Rydal Road. Turn right up Smithy Brow and almost at once
turn left along Nook Lane and very soon you will reach Low Sweden
Bridge, a charming picture. A path to the right following the course
of Scandale Beck leads up to High Sweden Bridge, then by a lane,
later to become an open track, ascending sharply towards the end to
the top of Scandale Pass.

From the top of the pass, take the path to the left, which runs to
the right of Little Hart Crag summit and on to the cairn near Dove
Crag, then turn due south in the direction of Ambleside and descend
down the long ridge of Scandale Fell and Low Pike to Low Sweden
Bridge. The views of Windermere and the surrounding districts
during the descent are magnificent.

From the bridge, return by the road as on the outward journey.
9 miles. (Moderate.)

Route 54. NAB SCAR. Take a Grasmere bus to Rydal. At
Rydal take the road on the right passing the church on your left.
After going through a gateway turn up to the left and through a
second gate to a path that rises between two walls and over a stile
on to the open fell. From here a path leads to the summit and to a
wonderful viewpoint with a panorama which includes eight lakes.
To continue, cross the stile close to the corner of the wall and follow
the path alongside the remains of a wall. Go down to the left in
the direction of Alcock Tarn, keeping it well to your right. Cross
Dunney Beck and follow a path which winds down to a high wall,
here it bends to the left and runs round three sides of an enclosure.
It then descends to a rough lane which is easily followed to Grasmere.
Here a bus can be taken back to Ambleside. *5 miles. (Moderate.)*

Route 55. ILL BELL. By Windermere bus to Troutbeck Bridge.
Then walk along a narrow unfenced road on the Windermere
side of the bridge, following the banks of the river for about a mile

before passing through a field on the right to join the Keswick–
Penrith road. When it joins the main road to Kirkstone Pass, turn
left and about a mile up the road strike off to the right by a narrow
road to Howe Farm. Passing the farm, the track continues between
two stone walls to the top of Garburn Pass. Just beyond the cairn
marking the summit of the pass a stone wall commences and rises
up the fell side on the left. Cross the wall and then keep close to
it until it almost reaches the top of Yoke. Continue to the summit
and then follow the summit ridge on to III Bell. There is a splendid
view of Windermere and the Kentmere Valley. Also of Thornthwaite
Crag and Harter Fell. To the west is the Coniston group, the
Scafell and Bowfell ranges, the Langdales and Helvellyn.

Continue north along the ridge on to Froswick for the fine view
of the crags on the east of III Bell, then drop down the slope to join
the footpath in the bottom. Follow the path towards and across
Troutbeck. Troutbeck is a long valley and often rather wet underfoot
in places. It is more interesting a little lower down after the track
crosses the beck on the left by a bridge about a mile down. Below
this the path passes through some pretty wooded country and
there are some pleasing cascades on the right.

The path goes through Troutbeck Park Farm and the remainder
of the route is along a narrow road to Troutbeck. Follow the signposts
to 'The Mortal Man'. A short distance beyond the Mortal Man Inn,
a lane starts on the right and rises sharply at first, and near the top
it bears to the right. Less than half a mile along here a signposted
footpath starts on the left; it leads round the side of Wansfell,
over the ridge, and down towards Ambleside to join the Stock Ghyll
road; turn left here to Ambleside. There are magnificent views of
Windermere from the Wansfell path. *14 miles. (Strenuous.)*

Route 56. CRINKLE CRAGS AND BOWFELL. Take the
Coniston bus to Colwith road end. On alighting follow the road
signposted to Colwith and, after crossing the river, fork left up the
road signposted 'To Wrynose'. Follow this past Little Langdale
Tarn, then, at the cattle grid fork left, drop to the farm at Fell Foot
and follow the long winding road to the top of Wrynose Pass. Near
the top is the Three Shire Stone, a tall column on the right of the
road bearing the word 'Lancashire'; this is the meeting of the three old
counties of Cumberland, Westmorland and Lancashire.

A path starts from the stone and rises up the fell side for about
half a mile. It continues to Red Tarn, but before reaching the tarn
strike off across the valley on the left and climb to the top of Cold
Pike. There is no apparent footpath until the summit is reached.

The path from the cairn continues in a north-westerly direction in
a line for the next summit, which is the first of the five Crinkle Crags.
Here fresh views burst upon us. Below is Eskdale with Devoke

Water in the background, behind lies Ravenglass and the Irish Sea, with the Isle of Man and Scotland probably in view. In front appears the Scafell group with its fine precipices; to the south is the Coniston group and Esthwaite Water; to the east, behind the Langdale Pikes, is High Street; farther north, towards Skiddaw, is the Helvellyn range.

The path crosses to the next peak, the second Crinkle. The direct route lies in front to the right of some steep crags, the climb is steep but short and entails a little scrambling on hands and knees, but is quite safe with proper precautions. There is an easier path to the summit round the left of the crags. This peak is the highest of the five.

You can continue over the top of the remaining three peaks or, if preferred, go round the foot of them to the left of the dip between Bowfell and Crinkle Crags, marked by a number of mountain pools named the Three Tarns; actually there are more. A rough steep climb of about 20 to 30 minutes, over scree and boulders, leads to the top of Bowfell.

The view from Bowfell is very extensive, and on an exceptionally clear day it is possible to see the Mountains of Mourne in Northern Ireland behind the south of the Isle of Man, the Welsh and Scottish hills, the Yorkshire and Lancashire hills and most of the Lakeland fells.

To descend, return to the Three Tarns, turn left, and a well-defined footpath, keeping to the left at first, leads down a long grassy tongue called The Band. There are two other footpaths starting between the summit of Bowfell and the Three Tarns, but they are not very easy to find; if you bear left about halfway down you will strike them.

There is no mistaking the path down The Band, as it drops to Stool End Farm where a road commences and leads to Dungeon Ghyll, where the bus can be caught back to Ambleside (fairly infrequent service). *Walking distance 12 miles. (Strenuous.)*

Route 57. RED TARN AND BROWNIE GHYLL. By Coniston bus to Colwith road end. Follow the previous route to the Three Shire Stone. Start along the same footpath and keep on the main track to Red Tarn.

There is an interesting diversion from here involving an extra hour, the ascent of Pike o'Blisco. Start climbing from the tarn, there is no definite footpath, and head directly for the summit. Half an hour's climbing should bring you to the top, which is very rocky, and a bit of scrambling may be necessary to reach the actual summit. The magnificent view includes the Crinkle Crags, Bowfell, Langdale Pikes and down the Langdale Valley to Windermere. Skiddaw is due north.

Return to Red Tarn, and continue beyond the tarn, along the path which, soon after, begins to drop sharply by Brownie Ghyll, crosses Oxendale Beck, and joins one of the tracks from the Three Tarns. Turn right to Stool End Farm, then by the road to Dungeon Ghyll for the bus to Ambleside. *9 miles. (Moderate.)*

AMBLESIDE TO KESWICK

A fairly new footpath above Thirlmere, opened by the Forestry Commission, has made it possible to walk most of the way by footpath between Ambleside and Keswick, thus avoiding a very busy road. Some of it is not yet marked on the maps, and it is easier to follow it from Ambleside.

Start along the main road from Ambleside, towards Keswick, then leave the road a short distance along by a footpath on the right, signposted to Rydal Hall. A good track goes to the right of the Hall to Grasmere. Don't descend to the village, but continue to the right of Winterseeds to a gate which may be locked. Climb over, to the foot of Tongue Gill, and descend the path over the beck to the Travellers Rest.

Dunmail Raise

The next mile is along the road up to the top of Dunmail Raise: opposite the summit cairn, cross a stile on the right and then another on the left and follow the track along the fell bottom, cross the beck by a footbridge below an attractive waterfall, and continue along the forest road above Thirlmere, crossing the Wythburn-Helvellyn footpath at right angles. Continue along the forest road until you leave the forest at the far end. Join a path coming down from Helvellyn and cross the main road at the Kings Head Inn.

Cross a stile on the opposite side of the road and continue through Great How Wood. Cross the Dam road and river at High Bridgend, and continue to the next plantation to pass Shoulthwaite Farm. Here you recross the main road, and a short distance to the right a sign-posted track starts and leads to Shaw Bank. Continue to the St. John's Church road and a footpath to the left takes you to Low Nest where you join the main road.

Castlerigg Stone Circle

By keeping right, a footpath takes you to Castlerigg Stone Circle, one of the largest in the Lake District, about 3,000 years old: from here a road leads into Keswick.

The other route to Keswick is to follow the main road from Low Nest up the hill towards Keswick, and turn left up a narrow road signposted to Rakefoot. This joins the Castlerigg road, and a few yards on the opposite side of this road, cross the bridge and continue down the path on the opposite side of the beck down to Springs Farm in the bottom. Continue along Springs Road and then into Keswick.

The distance is 18 miles, but this can be shortened at several places by taking the bus.

GRASMERE

Population: 1,100
Early Closing Day: Thursday
Tourist Information Centre: Broadgate News Agency 🛏
National Trust: Church Stile

ALTHOUGH GRASMERE IS COUPLED with Ambleside, it is four miles away on the road to Keswick and has its own entity. It is somewhat scattered and the actual village lies to the west of the main road and thus misses most of the traffic. It is a good centre for touring, being within easy reach of Ambleside, the Langdales and Keswick. Grasmere is much praised by those who prefer soft scenery to impressive grandeur, for it is romantically situated. The broad fine meadows stretching away from the lakeside to the fell slopes give Grasmere an endearing charm.

Wordsworth's Seat

Grasmere is famous for its literary associations. William Wordsworth lived at Dove Cottage, his first Lakeland home, from 1799 to 1808, and later the house was occupied by the de Quinceys. It is now open

Dove Cottage

to the public on weekdays and is much as it was when Wordsworth lived there, with the addition of a rich collection of MSS, portraits and other intimate mementoes of the poet. Other literary names associated with the village are Scott, Lamb, Coleridge, Southey, Ruskin, Matthew Arnold and Harriet Martineau. Wordsworth later lived at Rydal Mount, where he died, and on the roadside by the shores of Rydal is a mound, known as Wordsworth's Seat, where he was wont to sit.

The poet is buried in Grasmere church where his grave is marked by a simple slate slab. Nearby is the grave of Hartley Coleridge.

Grasmere lake is about a mile long and at its greatest width is about half a mile. Though small, it is in a beautiful setting and its western bank is gloriously wooded.

AROUND GRASMERE

Route 58. SILVER HOW. Starting from the church, proceed along the Keswick road until the Red Lion Hotel is reached; turn left, pass through a gate and follow the road past Allen Bank to Score Crag Farm; pass to the right of the latter and follow a footpath behind a wall. The path gradually disappears, so it is necessary to continue along the open fell, keeping to the right until a hollow is reached between two knobs. The left-hand knob is the summit of Silver How.

Descend in a line for Elterwater, observed below, until you strike a good footpath coming up from Langdale near Meg's Ghyll, turn left and follow this back to Grasmere. *4 miles. (Fairly easy.)*

Route 59. RED BANK. Follow the road from the village, keeping left from the church, round the west side of the lake, then about a mile from the church go up a by-road on the right past Hunting Stile House; farther on it becomes a footpath which rises to join the Red Bank road near the top of the rise. There is a grand view up the Langdale Valley from the top.

Return down the road towards Grasmere, cross the main road at the bottom and continue along a secondary road opposite or to Loughrigg Terrace, which goes round the foot of the lake. Take the next track to the left through a wood to cross the River Rothay between the lakes of Grasmere and Rydal and join the main road, which can be followed back to Grasmere. *6 miles. (Easy.)*

Route 60. ALCOCK TARN. Commence this walk at the Swan Hotel on the main road; go up the lane on the right of the hotel, cross the beck opposite the cottage and climb by the steps cut in the earth, follow these behind a wall and a plantation, then make for

Butter Crag, the craggy ridge on the left. A footpath from here leads to Alcock Tarn, skirts the right side of it, and continues past Lord Crag on the left, then drops to join a cart-road which continues down to join the main road beside Dove Cottage. *4 to 5 miles. (Easy.)*

Route 61. HELM CRAG. This is the prominent crag which overlooks Grasmere from the north, to the left of Dunmail Raise, and is famous for its Lion and Lamb Rock, and for another which resembles a lady playing the organ. It can be ascended directly from Grasmere, but the following is a more interesting, although longer, circular route.

By Keswick bus to Wythburn. From Wythburn Church start in the direction of Grasmere, then turn right down the first road on the right which goes round the head of the lake. At the first farm on the left turn up a lane which goes to the left of the farm, then drops to the Wythburn beck. Passing through a gateway, it becomes a mere fell track and follows the left side of the beck for some distance. As it rises there are some fine falls which are well worth seeing, especially after heavy rain.

Farther on the path levels and there are some Ice Age relics, the moraine heaps on the opposite side of the beck, similar to those found at the head of Ennerdale.

Near the head of the valley another footpath comes up Far Easedale on your left. Proceed a short distance down this path, then bear left by a footpath on to the first peak, Calf Crag, continue along the ridge over Gibson Knott on to Helm Crag. The first prominent rock on this crag is the one famous as the Old Lady Playing the Organ. It is very craggy round here, and care must be exercised. It is interesting to watch the traffic, like small toys, on the main road going over Dunmail Raise. A short distance towards Grasmere is another rock marking the top of the other crag, which is the Lion and Lamb Rock. The view over Grasmere and Windermere is very fine. A good footpath starts to the left, facing Grasmere, and this bears right down a rather steep slope to join the Far Easedale road below at the houses. Turn left and follow the road to Grasmere. *8 miles. (Moderate.)*

Route 62. ELTERWATER. By bus to Ambleside, then bus to Skelwith Bridge (Coniston or Elterwater bus).

Start by visiting Skelwith Force (Route 49). Continue along the road a short distance then take the footpath on the left signposted 'To Elterwater'. This path goes alongside Elterwater to Elterwater village. At the village turn right up the main road and then by the road signposted 'Grasmere by Red Bank' and follow this to the top of the rise. Part of the road can then be avoided by taking a footpath on the left to Hunting Stile, this later emerges into the road leading (left) back to Grasmere village. *Walking distance 5 miles. (Easy.)*

Route 63. GRISEDALE TARN. Bus or walk to the top of
Dunmail Raise road. A path starts by the beck on your right. Keep
this beck on your left and proceed up the valley for about 1½ miles,
moderate gradient, to Grisedale Tarn. A diversion on to the top of
Seat Sandal on your immediate right is worthwhile.

Descend to the tarn, pass round the other side over the outlet and
follow the track which rises up a short hill to a stone wall. It then
descends, there is a choice of two tracks, both meet near the bottom
and shortly after join the road at the foot of Dunmail Raise. *5 miles.
(Moderate.)*

Route 64. LOUGHRIGG TERRACE. Starting from the church,
take the road almost opposite, past Hayes Gardens, and keep left
round the far side of the lake. After about a mile and a half, a track
starts on the left and goes round the foot of the lake, this is Loughrigg
Terrace; it continues to the right of the river and along the shores
of Rydal. The river may be crossed near the outlet from Rydal
Water, or the terrace track may be followed another quarter-mile
to Pelter Bridge, which can be crossed, and the bus caught at the
main road back to Grasmere. *Walking distance 4 miles. (Easy.)*

Route 65. EASEDALE AND HIGH WHITE STONES. From the
church, pass Moss Grove Hotel to the corner of the main road,
crossing it and following the Easedale road on the opposite side for
a half-mile until a footbridge is reached on the left across the river.
Cross this bridge and follow the track through some fields, then up
the hillside to the left of Sour Milk Gill Falls, and on to Easedale Tarn.

There are two routes from here. One continues alongside the tarn
and rises by a beck at the top end, past Codale Tarn to Low White
Stones. A more interesting route is to leave the tarn about halfway
along and climb to a dip in the ridge, almost due south. The climb
is steep but short; near the top it bears right between two crags on to
the ridge. There are good views as the path continues along Blea
Rigg to the right of the summit of Low White Stones where it joins
the path from Codale Tarn, then it rises at a steady gradient to the
prominent cairn on Sergeant Man (2,414 feet).

Another half-mile north-west is the cairn marking the summit of
High Raise or High White Stones (2,500 feet), generally considered
to be the most central point in the Lake District; the view on a clear
day is magnificent, including most of the Lakeland fells, with Great
Gable especially prominent.

Proceeding due south over Thunacar Knott, the path leads to the
summit of Harrison Stickle, one of the Langdale Pikes. Descend to
the Dungeon Ghyll Hotel (see Route 52).

If desired, the return to Grasmere from Dungeon Ghyll may be
made by taking bus to Ambleside, and bus from there to Grasmere.

Or the bus can be taken as far as Elterwater and the return made on foot over Red Bank.

If no bus is available, the service being infrequent, or it is desired to return to Grasmere on foot, proceed down the valley by the old road, that is the road to the right of the main road starting from the New Hotel.

A little over a mile down the valley, the old road joins the new road at Robinson Place, a whitewashed farm building. A footpath starts behind the farm, ascends the fell side for a short distance, then bears right and cuts across the fell side, rising slightly all the time. Keep well up, bear left to the top of the ghyll above Chapel Stile, over the side of Silver How and down the far side (glorious views of Rydal and Grasmere lakes) to Grasmere village. *12 miles. (Fairly strenuous.)*

Route 66. GRISEDALE AND FAIRFIELD. About half a mile up the Dunmail Raise road from the Swan Hotel, a signposted track 'To Grisedale Tarn and Patterdale' starts just past the 'Travellers Rest'. At first the track goes between two stone walls, then soon opens out on to open fell. Keep to the left as it rises up along Tongue to the top of the pass where it crosses a stone wall, and Grisedale Tarn can be seen below.

Climb by the left side of the wall (turning right off the pass) for a short distance, when the path bears left and crosses the fell side. Soon it reaches rocky ground, intermingled with scree, and is difficult to follow. Make for the dip in the ridge on your right which can be seen a short distance ahead, Deepdale Hause, and, gaining the top of the ridge at this point, a good path follows the line of the ridge at an easy gradient to the top of St. Sunday Crag where Ullswater can be seen. Helvellyn is on the left or north and Striding Edge is the ridge below the summit.

Returning to Deepdale Hause, the path reaches the foot of what appears to be a formidable crag, but it looks worse than it is. The path winds round the rocks and after fifteen to twenty minutes' rough scrambling you find yourself suddenly on the top; the path continues round the fell side to the left, and a few minutes later the top of Fairfield is reached.

There are several cairns on the top and it is not easy to decide which is the actual summit, but the view from each is very extensive. You look down the greater part of the length of Windermere and Coniston lakes, with several other smaller lakes also in view. Almost every well-known peak, with the exception of Skiddaw and Saddleback, which are hidden by Helvellyn, can be seen on a clear day.

To return to Grasmere, proceed in the direction between Windermere and Coniston lakes, along a well-worn footpath which drops to Rydal Fell. The path rises slightly over Rydal Fell, from where

is a good view of Grasmere, then it drops to Heron Pike and a small
tarn, Alcock Tarn, comes into view below on the right. To the left
of the tarn is a stone wall; drop down towards this to strike a footpath
which goes down to the left of this wall, later dropping sharply
down the wooded slopes of Brackenfell with Dumney Beck coming
in on the left near the bottom. Finally, it sweeps down in a big
semicircle to join a road which leads to the main road near Dove
Cottage, and then to Grasmere village. *9 miles. (Strenuous.)*

Route 67. HELVELLYN. Because it is one of the four Lakeland
peaks over the 3,000 feet contour, and one of the most central,
Helvellyn is one of the most popular fells in the Lake District. It
can be climbed from Grasmere by following out the previous route
to Grisedale Tarn, then ascending the winding path up the side of
Dollywaggon Pike, from the top of which is only a very short distance
on to Helvellyn. This can also be used in the opposite direction.

Take the Keswick bus to Wythburn. The path starts to the left of
Wythburn Church, at first being a fairly wide pony-track, later
narrowing, but it cannot be missed as it winds up the fell side to the
summit of Helvellyn. This is actually the shortest route up this fell.

There is a tablet on the summit indicating the various peaks which
can be seen. Much of Ullswater can be seen to the north-east.
There is also a stone wall built in the shape of an X as a shelter from
the winds. The most interesting part of Helvellyn is Striding Edge,
a narrow knife-like edge on the Ullswater side of the summit. With
ordinary care, the edge is quite safe, although accidents have
happened and it is inadvisable for the stranger to go alone.

From the shelter, begin the descent in a south-easterly direction,
keeping clear of the crags on your immediate left. A few yards
down you pass the memorial stone to Charles Gough, who died
from exposure in 1805; his faithful dog watched by his master's body
for three months until the remains were discovered. Walter Scott
describes the event in the poem 'I Climbed the Dark Brows of
Mighty Helvellyn', and Canon Rawnsley wrote a story, *The Dog
of Helvellyn.* In 1890, Canon Rawnsley and Miss Frances Cobbe
erected the monument to the memory of the dog.

The path drops sharply down rough scree from the monument,
then begins to rise. There is a rock about six feet high to climb,
but it is not very difficult, and is more awkward in the opposite
direction; after this there is quite an easy walk along the ridge, with
a second path a little lower down on the left for the more timid.

At the far end is a grassy slope, the path continues in the same
direction and soon after begins a steady fall in the direction of
Ullswater, which appears in front. Keep right halfway down at the
fork (the left side leads to Glenridding), and this will bring you out
near the foot of Grisedale Valley.

To return to Grasmere, turn up the valley and follow the track up Grisedale Pass to Grisedale Tarn. Turn left at the tarn, crossing the beck at the outlet, then, after another very short rise, the path descends towards Grasmere. There is a track either side of Tongue Ghyll, both lead to Grasmere and there is little to choose excepting that the right-hand route is easier to find near the bottom. *16 miles. (Strenuous.)*

Route 68. BLEA TARN AND WATENDLATH. Take a Keswick bus to Wythburn. Start by the road which goes round the head of Thirlmere, and at about a half-mile leave the road ½ mile beyond Stenkin Farm on the left by a foot-track which rises by Dub Gill (very rough) to Harrop Tarn. The ground between here and Blea Tarn is liable to be boggy and preparations should be made (carry spare socks). The path passes Blea Tarn and come on to a fell overlooking Watendlath; descend to the hamlet, then go over Grange Fell on the other side of the tarn to Rosthwaite or follow the road by Ashness Bridge to the Borrowdale road. Bus to Keswick. *Walking distance to Rosthwaite 7 miles. (Moderate.)*

CONISTON

Population: 1,000
Early Closing Day: Wednesday

CONISTON IS A CHARMING VILLAGE situated at the foot of Coniston Old Man and Yewdale Crags; the latter appear to tower above the village, making the scene very impressive. The Church Beck flows through the centre and on into Coniston Lake, which is a good half-mile from the village. The route to the lake is by the Crown Hotel and then by a footpath through the fields. Coniston is a good centre for the Lancashire fells, Duddon, Ambleside and Windermere being within easy reach.

Coniston is closely associated with John Ruskin; the house where he lived and died, Brantwood, is on the opposite side of the lake, about one and a half miles from the head. He was buried in Coniston churchyard and over his grave stands a tall, beautifully carved cross. It carries the simple inscription 'John Ruskin. 1819–1900', and the carvings are representative of Ruskin's works and interests.

Ruskin Museum

The Ruskin Museum in Yewdale Road contains many interesting and valuable exhibits, including drawings, manuscripts and other articles associated with John Ruskin.

Coniston Water is over five miles long, and an average of half a mile wide. It is best approached from the foot of the lake, as the scenery is rather tame at that end and becomes grander and more beautiful as the head of the lake is approached; the fells in view include the Old Man, Wetherlam, Helvellyn, Fairfield and the Red Screes.

Many attempts on the world water speed record were made on the lake by Donald Campbell, who was killed on Coniston Water while travelling at 310 m.p.h. in *Bluebird* on 4th January, 1967. A memorial commemorates him.

AROUND CONISTON

Route 69. TARN HOWS. This is one of the prettiest lakes in the Lake District. It is an artificial lake made by damming up some marshes. The actual name is Highlow Tarn, but it is more frequently known as Tarn Hows, which is the name of a nearby farm, meaning the hill by the lake.

From Coniston village, follow the cinder footpath round the head of the lake, take the first road on the left signposted 'Hawkshead', for ¼ mile to foot of steep hill. Follow narrow road on left for few yards, then a bridle track on right which leads up to Tarn Hows.

Another good route, following footpaths almost all the way, is to start from the village, along the Ambleside road, and turn down the first road on the right which forms a triangle with the roads around the village. A short distance along this road a footpath signposted 'High Yewdale' is on the left. Follow this until you reach a narrow lane: turn right down the lane for about fifty yards, then left through a gate and along a bridle road up the hill. There is a good view of Coniston from here. Keep near the side of the wood, on your right, until you reach Tarn Hows Farm. Continue past the farm along a narrow road to the east until you join another tarred road which leads up to Tarn Hows.

There are several different routes but all eventually lead to the Tarn. Its shores are well wooded, and in the background are the Langdale Pikes, the Fairfield Fells, Wansfell and Ill Bell.

Follow the road round to the right for a short distance and cross a low stone wall up a small fell; here there is a wonderful view including most of Coniston Water, and a panorama of fells as far north as Saddleback.

There is a track round the east side of the lake which joins the road from Borwick Lodge into Oxenfell main road, but a more pleasant walk is to return to the tarn from the viewpoint, walk round the foot to the dam, then drop down Glen Mary by Tom Gill, crossing the latter halfway down by a footbridge.

The main road is reached at the bottom. Turn left along this road,

Coniston   Yew Tree Farm

Newby Bridge   South of Windermere

Ambleside   Old Bridge House

and opposite the first farm on the right, a footpath (signposted to Coniston) starts from the gateway, passes through several fields before joining the road near Coniston.

Another footpath starts farther along the road from Tom Gill, just past the Tilberthwaite road end. It starts from a stile on the right and proceeds almost parallel with the road nearly to Coniston, about 2 miles. If desired, one of the infrequent buses may be taken from Tom Gill to Coniston. *Walking distance to foot of Tom Gill, 3 miles (excluding visit to viewpoint, ½ mile). (Easy.)*

Route 70. TILBERTHWAITE GHYLL. By Ambleside bus to Tilberthwaite road end (1½ miles). If you prefer to walk, or there is no convenient bus, a good footpath leads through the woods to the left of the main road: this joins the main road at Tilberthwaite road end. On alighting start along the secondary road on the left (west) and about one and a half miles along, a footpath, the second on the left, leaves the road and winds up past some slate quarries. It then drops sharply to cross the beck, Tilberthwaite Ghyll, by a footbridge. It was possible to proceed up the Ghyll by a succession of footbridges, but these have now collapsed and are unlikely to be replaced. A good view of the Ghyll can be obtained from a footbridge at the bottom. To reach the top, climb up the bank on the right until a good path is reached. This leads along the fell side, high above the Ghyll, to a footbridge over the falls. Return by the same path to Tilberthwaite Cottages and back to the main road for the bus to Coniston. *4 miles. (Easy.)*

Route 71. CONISTON OLD MAN. Start from the Black Bull Hotel by the road signposted to the Y.H.A., this follows the course of the Church Beck for over a mile to the Copper Mines, where the hostel is situated. From the hostel keep left and follow the track to Low Water. Much mining is carried on at the slate quarries around here and the fell side is full of ugly scars.

A footpath from Low Water bears left beneath the crags of the Old Man, then rises sharply to the summit. The view is one of great contrasts, the ruggedness of the north and the rich woodlands of the south giving it much variety. Almost the whole of Coniston Lake is in view, and farther south, Morecambe Bay and the Duddon Estuary. To the north and east are most of the principal fells, including the Scafell, Skiddaw, Helvellyn and High Street groups.

To return, either proceed due south by Cove Quarries to join the Walna Scar road, or descend to Goats Water on the west for a closer view of the magnificent crags on Dow Crag. A path from the tarn follows the course of the beck which flows from it and joins the Walna Scar road, along which turn to the left for Coniston. *6 miles. (Strenuous.)*

F

Route 72. WETHERLAM AND SWIRL HOW. Follow the directions in Route 70 to the top of Tilberthwaite Gill. From the footbridge over the falls continue along the path that rises and winds to the top of Wetherlam (2,502 feet). The view includes the Brathay Valley leading down to Windermere, Elterwater, Little Langdale Tarn and the Langdale Pikes. Crossing a deep depression in a south-westerly direction, there is a sharp rise on to Swirl How, another grand viewpoint.

It is worth while making a slight diversion from Swirl How along the ridge to the north, on to Carrs, about ten minutes' walk, for the grand view down the Duddon Valley. From Swirl How the way now lies due south along a pleasant grassy ridge, very easy walking, for nearly two miles, with grand views on either side, until the short easy rise to the summit of Coniston Old Man.

The return to Coniston is to continue along the track as it descends to the Walna Scar road and turn along it to the left. *12 miles. (Strenuous.)*

Route 73. WALNA SCAR AND DOW CRAG. Leave Coniston by the road which goes under the railway bridge near the station, continue up the road, which becomes a rough pony-track, to the top of Walna Scar Pass. Turn right at the top and climb to the top of the first peak, which is Brown Pike. Continue in a northerly direction along an easy rise on to Dow Crag. Beware of the many crags which are below the summit to the east, facing Coniston Old Man, which is immediately opposite. There is a very fine view of the Duddon Valley from the summit.

To continue, proceed a short distance to the north to pass beyond the crags, then bear right and drop to the hollow above the head of Goats Water, climb up the grassy slope on the other side to the top of the Old Man. For the descent to Coniston, see the previous route. *9 miles. (Fairly strenuous.)*

Route 74. SATTERTHWAITE AND GRISEDALE. By Ulverston bus to Water Yeat, turn left to cross the river, then left again along the road through High Nibthwaite. Almost through the village, start along a fell track on the right which runs parallel with the lake shore for some distance to Parkamoor, bear right just before reaching the latter and follow the track over the fells to Satterthwaite. Much of the land has been afforested in recent years. Turn left up the road for one and a half miles to Grisedale, this narrow road goes through some beautiful country.

Grisedale Hall is a Nature Conservancy with a museum, theatre and nature trails. Almost opposite Grisedale Hall, a forestry track starts, rising up the fell side. It is signposted to Coniston. After about a half mile, take right-hand track and keep straight over the rise, crossing another main track, before descending to join the road at Bank Ground. It is easy to take a wrong turning in the wood and a map and a compass will be a good help. Turn right up this road for a few yards, then left at the fork which leads past Tent House, once the home of Tennyson, and goes round the head of the lake, past the Waterhead Hotel into Coniston. *Walking distance 12 miles. (Moderate.)*

Route 75. BORWICK AND OXENFELL. By bus to Boon Crag Wall Post Box (Coniston terminus of Ambleside bus). Follow the road towards Ambleside for a mile to Borwick Lodge, turn left up a narrow road on the left which rises gradually for some distance. Near the top, glorious views unfold which include the Langdale Pikes, Bowfell range and Tarn Hows on the left; there is another small tarn on the immediate right which is called Arnside Tarn. The road gradually drops to join the main Oxenfell road where the bus can be caught back to Coniston.

The route can be extended if desired by crossing the main road and proceeding along another lane which goes up to High Oxon, and down the other side to Hodge Close. Turn left to Holme Ground and then along the road by Yewdale Beck, across Shepherds Bridge on to the main road at High Yewdale. Bus to Coniston. *Walking distances to Oxenfell, 4½ miles; by Holme Ground to High Yewdale, 8 miles. (Both easy.)*

Route 76. BLEA TARN AND DUNGEON GHYLL. By Ambleside bus to Tilberthwaite road end. Start along the road on the left to the cottages at Tilberthwaite, keep along the road to High Tilberthwaite, then take the open track on the left round the foot of Low Fell to Fell Foot Farm. Upon crossing the river before the farm turn right to the gate, then left along the road which leads past Blea Tarn to Dungeon Ghyll (see Route 51). Bus to Skelwith Bridge or Ambleside, then bus to Coniston. *Walking distance 7 miles. (Moderately easy.)*

Route 77. LICKLE VALLEY. By bus as far as Woodland. Proceed along the road to the village, turn left down the main road a few yards, then right along a secondary road, turn right at the next junction for about a mile, cross over a track coming up from Broughton Mills, and continue up the right of the River Lickle. Soon it becomes an open pony-track and proceeds along the fell side above the beck, joining the track on the far side higher up. It next crosses open fell and it is not too easy to follow in parts.

Just over a mile of open fell land, the track joins the Walna Scar track coming up from the Duddon Valley, follow this to the right to the top of the pass and down the other side into Coniston. *Walking distance 9 miles. (Moderate.)*

Route 78. WALNA SCAR AND WRYNOSE. Start up the road beneath the railway bridge near the station and continue along this road over Walna Scar Pass into the Duddon Valley. Upon reaching the first farm, Long House, in the Duddon Valley, take the track to the right over the beck, Long House Ghyll, to the next farm at Tongue House. A footpath from there crosses Tarn Beck, and half a mile beyond joins the road coming up the Duddon Valley from Seathwaite.

Follow the road up the valley. At the first bridge on the left over the river, Birks Bridge, look beneath the bridge from upstream to see the famous Giant's Leg.

Continue up the valley to Cockley Beck and then over Wrynose Pass to Fell Foot, the farm at the bottom of the pass. Turn right at the farm to follow a road which crosses the river, keep left at the next fork keeping fairly close to Little Langdale Tarn on your left, to a crossroad; continue along the opposite road over Pierce How Beck to Stand End and still keep in the same direction, due east, with the River Brathay on your left, to High Park, where the road bears right to go south-east to join the main road on Oxenfell. The bus may be caught to Coniston from this point. *Walking distance to Oxenfell, 15 miles. (Moderate.)*

TOURS FROM CONISTON

Tour 13. Around Coniston Water. *14 miles.*

Tour 14. Torver, Blawith, turn left at Lowick Bridge to Gawthwaite, Grisebeck, Broughton-in-Furness, Torver, Coniston. *24 miles.*

Tour 15. Hawkshead, then by one of three roads, by Grisedale and Satterthwaite; Thwaite Head and Rusland, or Graythwaite and Newby Bridge, all leading to Greenodd, then to Spark Bridge, and Blawith to Coniston. *27 miles.*

Tour 16. Hawkshead, Esthwaite Water, Graythwaite, Newby Bridge, Lindale, Grange-over-Sands, Flookburgh, Cark, Low Wood, Spark Bridge, Blawith, Coniston. *42 miles.*

PATTERDALE and ULLSWATER

Population: 700
Early Closing Day: Friday

ULLSWATER IS NEARLY NINE MILES in length, set in the midst of the most superb scenery and vying with Derwentwater as the most

beautiful of the English lakes. Because of its delightful setting in
some of the richest and grandest scenery of Lakeland it is often
compared with the Swiss lakes and the Scottish lochs.

At the Pooley Bridge, or northern end of the lake, the shores are
somewhat pastoral, intermixed with woods and groves that come
down to the water's edge; in the middle reach—Ullswater has three
distinct reaches—the scenery becomes bolder and the fells rise sheer
out of the lake; whilst at the Patterdale end Ullswater presents a
picture of mountain beauty equal to anything found elsewhere in
the Lake District.

Pooley Bridge consists of several hotels and houses, but there is
not a great deal of interest there. Motor yachts start at the pier for
a most enjoyable sail up Ullswater. At first the scenery is not
remarkable, but after about two miles the view of the middle reach
opens up and the scenery becomes more picturesque. Soon the boat
enters a bay to call at Howtown, and a good plan is to land here and
walk the remaining six miles along the lake shore to Patterdale, for
it is along this path that the beauty of Ullswater is seen at its best.

Longest Reach

The scenery after the boat leaves Howtown for the third and longest
reach of the lake is magnificent. At the far end is Helvellyn with
St. Sunday Crag on the left. On the immediate right as we pass up
the lake is Glencoyne and the well-wooded Stybarrow Crag
descending into the lake. Opposite, on our left, is Place Fell, which
descends almost to the water edge. Kirkstone Pass can be observed
right at the head of the valley to the left of St. Sunday Crag. The
landing stage is about half a mile from the head of the lake opposite
Glenridding.

Glenridding is just a small hamlet consisting of two hotels, a few
houses and shops, snack bars (not always open), and a pay car park.

Charming Situation

Patterdale village is a mile higher up the valley and is one of the
most charmingly situated in the country. A great deal of the land
around Ullswater is now National Trust property, the most notable
being the Gowbarrow Fell Estate and Glencoyne Wood. The
Gowbarrow Estate of over 700 acres includes Gowbarrow Fell, which
is a good point for viewing the lake, and Aira Force, a beautiful
waterfall of seventy feet, set in a glen of great natural beauty; it is
reached within a few minutes' walk of the road where the road from
Troutbeck joins the lakeside. There is a café and a good car park
at this point. About half a mile up the hill towards Troutbeck is a
stile on the right. By starting from here and dropping down to the
falls by the footpath, and then continuing down towards the lake, a
delightful walk will be experienced with glorious views all the way.

Gowbarrow

Gowbarrow is one of the most beautiful natural pleasure grounds
in the country and is familiar to all who read Wordsworth's poems;
it was the sight of the vast number of daffodils growing here in the
spring that inspired him to write:

'Ten thousand saw I at a glance,
Tossing their heads in sprightly dance.

The National Trust wrote of Gowbarrow: 'No tourist, British
or American, misses the sight of Aira Force; but none heretofore
have had the right to roam at will over the Deer Park, to walk through
the lovely meadows on the south side of the glen, or to move
downward through the grove of dark pine towards the shore on that
side of the stream. Few have climbed the rocky steps of Yew Crag, or
passed up the huntsman's path on the mountain breast and met the
red deer face to face on Gowbarrow Fell. None have been able to
take a boat on the shore beneath Lyulph's Tower and gain at their
leisure the views of Stybarrow and Glencoyne, and the head of the
lake which Turner has made famous. Take it all in all, there is no
single fell in the Lake District where such grouping of mountain
and parkland and waterfall can be obtained. From the summit,
1,578 feet, one gains views of Skiddaw and Blencathra to the
north-west, of Penrith Beacon and the land round Carlisle to the
north, of the Cross Fell Range and High Street to the north and east,
with Hallin Fell and the hills of Martindale and Place Fell and Baeda
Fell in the foreground across the lake, while to the south-west the
masses of St. Sunday Crag and Helvellyn dominate the nearer slopes
of Glenridding, and Black Crag is seen across the hollow park-like
grounds of Glencoyne.'

Since that was written, all this land has been acquired by the Trust
and opened to the public.

Ullswater has many associations with William Wordsworth, for
his grandparents on his father's side resided near Penrith; his wife
also belonged to Penrith. At Yanwath, on the road to Penrith, is
The Grotto, which was occupied by Thomas Wilkinson, a Quaker
friend of Wordsworth, where the latter often stayed.

AROUND PATTERDALE

Route 79. AIRA FORCE. A bus from Patterdale may be taken to
the entrance to the falls at the junction of the Troutbeck—Pooley
Bridge road. Two other tracks start from the car park just beyond the
café, the right-hand one by the river is the longer of the two but is
he more picturesque. The tower on the right as you leave the road

for the falls is called Lyulph's Tower; it is a square, ivy-mantled
building, and harmonizes with the surrounding wooded countryside.
Notwithstanding its appearance, it is no relic of the past, but was
built about a century ago as a hunting lodge. ½ *mile from road.*
(Easy.)

Route 80. BOARDALE. Start from the Kirkstone side of Patterdale
Post Office; just round the corner, a road starts on the left, crosses
the river and over the valley to Rooking. Here a pony-track on
the right rises sharply up the fell side to Boardale Hause and then
drops down the other side and continues down the fairly long valley of
Boardale. In about three miles the track forks: take the left fork
and follow it until it is about to cross Howe Grain Beck. Then take
the unfenced track on the left, keeping right until it reaches the lake
side. The next four miles along the side of the lake is one of the
prettiest walks in the country and undoubtedly the place for seeing
Ullswater at its best. Shortly after leaving the lake, a road branches
to the right, crosses the valley and river above the head of the lake,
joining the main road near the Patterdale Hotel. *12 miles. (Moderate.)*

Route 81. PLACE FELL. Follow Route 80 to the top of the pass,
Boardale Hause, above Rooking, then, instead of dropping down to
Boardale, turn left along a path, which ascends to the top of the
ridge on Place Fell. There are several stone cairns on the top, which
is a very fine viewpoint.

To descend, make for the cairn in the direction of Penrith, which
should be seen (N.E.) in the distance, and continue past the cairn to
the edge of the steep lower part of the slope. A narrow path
commences close to a small gully and descends obliquely through the
bracken to join the Boardale road near Nettleslack Farm. Either
follow the route as described in Route 80 along the lake side to
Patterdale, or continue from Boardale, keeping right at the first
junction to Howtown, returning in the steamer to Patterdale. *Distance
to Howtown, 6 miles. (Fairly strenuous.)*

Route 82. ANGLE TARN. Follow Route 80 to the top of
Boardale Hause, then turn right along a well-marked path between
two grassy elevations. Soon the path reaches higher ground and a
grand view appears. Continue along the side of The Pikes and soon
you arrive at Angle Tarn.

The path continues to rise to the right of several crags, then passes
along the side of Rest Dod towards the summit of The Knott. It
is not necessary to go right to the summit, for a winding footpath
leads down on the right half a mile below the summit to Hayeswater.
Cross the Ghyll near the foot of the tarn, and a footpath on the left
of the Ghyll leads down to Low Hartsop, a delightful old-world

village. From here, the return to Patterdale is along the road or by
bus. *8 miles (Low Hartsop to Patterdale is 2½ miles).*
(Moderate.)

Route 83. KIDSTY PIKE AND HIGH STREET NORTH. By
Windermere bus to Low Hartsop. Then start along the road with
the river on your right, through Low Hartsop, after which it becomes
a rough track, and care should be taken not to take the right-hand
fork which leads up Pasture Beck. The track crosses the river and
then bears left following the beck up to Hayeswater.

As soon as the tarn comes into view a footpath starts on the left,
descends to cross the beck by a footbridge a few yards below the
tarn, then over a stile and up a winding path to the top of The Knott.
At the top, leave the path and pass over to the peak on the left and
ten minutes' walking should bring you to the top of Kidsty Pike.
The view includes a small portion of Haweswater, Shap and the
Yorkshire Fells.

Next make your way round to the summit of High Raise to the
north and follow the track along High Street over Raven How and
Red Crag. About two miles along, a track on the left descends to
pass through a stone wall by a gate, then down a long tongue, Steel
Knotts, towards a white building observed in the valley near to
Ullswater. At the bottom of Steel Knotts a visit should be made
to Old Martindale Church. Follow the road down towards Sandwick,
turn left at the point where the road is about to cross Howe Grain
Beck, and return to Patterdale as described in Route 80. *14 miles.*
(Strenuous.)

Route 84. HIGH STREET AND THORNTHWAITE CRAG.
As previous route to Kidsty Pike. From the Pike, retrace your path
a short distance, then wind round to the left in a big semi-circle to a
stone wall. Follow the direction of the wall due south for about two
miles, where the wall is replaced by a fence. This bears sharp right
after a short distance and a wall can then be followed to the top
of Thornthwaite Crag, easily recognized by the tall stone column
which stands on the summit.

The main feature of the view is Windermere, almost the whole
of the lake being visible. There is also a grand fell view which includes
the Coniston range, Black Combe, the Bowfell group, Scafell,
Langdale Pikes, Great Gable, a small portion of Pillar, the Helvellyn
range, and, closer at hand, Ill Bell and the Mardale Harter Fell.

A long rough descent, north-west, leads to the top of Caudale
Moor. The path drops sharply down this valley at first, but lower
down it becomes very easy as it follows Pasture Beck to Low Hartsop
where the bus can be caught at the main road to Patterdale. *10 miles.*
(Strenuous.)

Route 85. HAWESWATER. Follow the route as previously described to the top of Kidsty Pike. Drop down the side of the fell by a footpath towards the lake, Haweswater, which can be seen below. This used to be a very pretty lake with an interesting old church and several farms, but since Manchester Water Works raised the level of the lake shortly before the Second World War, all these buildings have disappeared below the waters and much of the charm of Haweswater has been lost. There is a footpath round one side of the lake, and a road runs along the eastern shores on which is Haweswater Hotel, which replaced the old Dun Bull at Mardale, now under water.

On arriving at the lake side, cross the bridge over the Riggindale Beck and follow the path to the head of the lake where it crosses the river and a pony-track. Take the right fork over Gatescarth Pass dropping down the far side into the Long Sleddale Valley.

At the first farm, the road improves and half a mile farther a road branches to the right and crosses the river to Hill Hole Farm. A track from here leads to the next farm, Toms Howe, and then rises slightly alongside of Cocklaw Fell, passing Skeggles Water on the left. It then gradually descends down Staveley Head Fell to the village of Staveley; there is a good pony-track all the way from Toms Howe.

Staveley is on the main road between Kendal and Windermere, and the journey to Windermere station can be made by bus, and then the bus from there over Kirkstone Pass to Patterdale. *Walking distance to Staveley, 16 miles. (Strenuous.)*

Route 86. HELVELLYN. The ascent from Thirlmere and the view is described in Route 67.

From Patterdale, start up a road opposite the Ullswater Hotel, keeping Glenridding Beck on the left all the way. It follows this road for one and half miles to Greenside Smelting Mills. From here, keep to the left along the course of the main beck to Kepplecove Tarn, now empty, and then a path zigzags to the top of the ridge; bear left and this leads to the top of Helvellyn.

A shorter route is to start along the same road, but bear left at the first junction to cross Glenridding Beck, and a footpath starts soon after and rises up the fell side to Red Tarn. Here you can either keep left over Striding Edge or cross over below the tarn and go up the winding path of Swirrel Edge.

The third route from Patterdale is to start near the church by the road signposted to Grisedale Pass and Grasmere. Follow this for about four miles; it is quite easy excepting for the climb at the last half-mile to the top of the pass at Grisedale Tarn. A path from the tarn starts to the right and zigzags up the side of Dollywaggon Pike, rather a steep, stiffish climb, but from the summit of the Pike it is only a few minutes' walk to the top of Helvellyn.

The most popular route is to start up the Grisedale Valley from Patterdale, for about a mile, then cross the river on your right by a footbridge. A footpath starts to rise up the fell side, fairly steep in parts until it reaches a stone wall at the top. The path now reaches a narrow rocky ledge called Striding Edge. Great care must be exercised in crossing this, and it should be avoided in wild or frosty weather. There is a drop of about ten feet at the far end which requires care, then there is a rough steep climb up the scree to the shelter on the top of Helvellyn. This is an ideal route for those wanting a little excitement, but it is quite safe in good weather; boots are essential for safety. This route is described in the reverse direction in Route 67.

Any of these routes can be used for the descent to Ullswater, but the most interesting is that over Striding Edge (see above). *Distance up Helvellyn, by Grisedale Tarn or Kepplecove Tarn, 6 miles. By Red Tarn, 4 miles. (Strenuous.)*

Route 87. STICKS PASS. There is not a great deal to recommend this route, excepting that it is the shortest and quickest way of reaching Thirlmere. Start by the road described in the first paragraph of the previous route to Greenside Smelting Mill, then turn right up the zigzagging path by Greenside Lead Mines. Above here it joins another track which comes up from Glencoyne and rises to the top of the ridge. The route was marked by white sticks but few remain. It drops down the far side to the main road at Stanah, and here the bus can be caught to Keswick or Windermere. *6 miles. (Moderate.)*

Route 88. ST. SUNDAY CRAG. Follow the road from the church up Grisedale Pass to the tarn. A footpath starts from the tarn and rises diagonally along the side of Fairfield on the opposite side of the beck from which you climbed the pass. Soon it reaches rough scree and is difficult to follow, but by making for the depression in front, Deepdale Hause, the path will be picked up again and it now rises up the grassy ridge to the summit of St. Sunday Crag.

A few yards to the east of the summit a good view of Ullswater is obtained, and in the opposite direction from the summit the crags of Fairfield are seen to an advantage. To the north-west is Helvellyn and Striding Edge, and through the gap between Fairfield and Helvellyn appear Coniston and Scafell groups of mountains, and to the east the High Street and Pennine Chain.

The descent is made in a direct line down the grassy slope towards the head of Ullswater, and the path joins the road near the church. *8 miles. (Moderately strenuous.)*

Route 89. FAIRFIELD. Start from the church, up the Grisedale Pass road for a quarter-mile, where a footpath starts on the left, and then by the ridge to the top of St. Sunday Crag. Continue down the ridge on the other side to Deepdale Hause, then up the path by the crags on to Fairfield (see Route 66). An alternative is to follow the pass to Grisedale Tarn. At the stone wall above the tarn, turn left and follow a footpath direct to the summit of Fairfield (approximately 20 minutes from tarn). Fairfield has a fairly flat summit with three cairns, which can be confusing in a mist.

Leave Fairfield in a south-easterly direction, with Windermere in the distance on your immediate right, and cross over to Hart Crag. Turn sharp left to face north-east, and drop down the ridge to Hartsop above How, with Deepdale Beck on your left and Brotherswater on your right. The path continues down the slope to join the main road a mile below Brotherswater. Patterdale is a mile down the road. *10 miles. (Strenuous.)*

Route 90. HAWESWATER FROM HOWTOWN. By steamer to Howtown. Pass through a gate by the side of Howtown Hotel, and enter the Fusedale Valley. Keep the beck on your right for a short distance, then cross it. The farm track which recrosses the beck higher up becomes a footpath. Keep the stream on your right then bear to the left to cross the ridge at Weather Hill. There is a good view from this point which includes part of Ullswater on one side and Haweswater on the other. Many of the Lakeland peaks are hidden, but Coniston Old Man can be seen between Fairfield and Red Screes, while much of the Pennine Chain, including Cross Fell, appears to the east.

Drop down the fell side towards Haweswater, striking Measand Beck lower down; there are some waterfalls near the bottom. Turn left and follow the lake shore to the dam at the foot of the lake and join the road at Naddle Gate. Follow the road to the left to Bampton. Bus to Penrith and then to Patterdale. *8 miles. (Moderate.)*

Section 4

Western Lake District

THE WESTERN LAKE DISTRICT is a most neglected part, both by books and by visitors; this is probably because, unlike the other parts, it contains no towns or large villages. There are no places of amusement apart from the village hall and buildings are very scattered. Yet the Western Lake District contains some of the finest scenery in the whole of the area.

The visitor who wants to escape from the crowds, from the noise and bustle of the busy world, who wishes to seek the peace and quietness of the countryside, cannot do better than make one of these valleys a centre for the holiday, for it is here that he will come into close contact with the real Lakelander and the true spirit of the fells. It is possible to wander on these fells for a whole day and meet only an occasional farmer with his dog rounding up the sheep.

Five Valleys

The Western Lake District contains five valleys; they are the Duddon, Eskdale, Wasdale, Ennerdale and Buttermere; two of them possess no natural lake. They are valleys of great contrast. The Duddon and Eskdale are full of charm and beauty, Wasdale is a vivid contrast, being wild and magnificent. There are some who do not like this valley, considering it deep and gloomy; others think there is nothing like it, the more one visits it the greater its attraction. Ennerdale is wild in a different aspect and there are many who consider that the Liza Valley at the head of Ennerdale is the finest of all the Lakeland valleys, although the afforestation scheme has done much to spoil it. The Buttermere Valley differs again from all the rest, it has a quiet gentle beauty which appeals to many lovers of natural scenery. Buttermere Lake itself, often calm like a huge mirror with the grand background formed by Fleetwith and Haystacks, is a favourite subject for artists and photographers.

THE DUDDON VALLEY

THE DUDDON VALLEY is very picturesque. The River Duddon rises near the top of Wrynose Pass, close by the Three Shire Stone, and from here to the sea at Foxfield it once formed the boundary line between Cumberland and Lancashire. It runs through wild and picturesque country and is worthwhile following from source to sea. It was a favourite haunt of William Wordsworth, who wrote no less than thirty-four sonnets about it.

From its source to Cockley Beck the country is very desolate, but below it quickly changes as the valley broadens and is more cultivated. Much of it has been planted by the Forestry Commission. At Birks Bridge the river narrows and flows steeply down between the sides of a deep and narrow gorge. Beneath the bridge, seen by looking down river, is a remarkable rock, formed by the water into the shape of a leg and known as 'The Giant's Leg'. About a quarter of a mile up the river from Birks Bridge is a large car park and a number of picnic tables.

The river next passes through well-wooded country in which the silver birch predominates, and continues through the beautiful Wallabarrow Gorge to Seathwaite.

Wonderful Walker

Seathwaite is famous for its simple little church, occupying the site of an old chapel which for many years was under the ministration of 'Wonderful Walker'. The Rev. Robert Walker was curate of Seathwaite for over sixty years and, although his salary never exceeded £50 per year—his wife had a private income of £40 per annum—he was able to give his children a good education, and earned extra money by becoming, as required, teacher, lawyer and doctor, and by doing other odd jobs which included making home-brewed beer which he sold to his congregation on a Sunday afternoon. When he died, at the age of 93, in June, 1802, he left £2,000. His grave is to be found in the churchyard.

There is a pleasant excursion from Seathwaite. Instead of following the road towards Ulpha, follow a track which starts near the church signposted 'To the Bridge' and crosses the river to Low Crag, then proceed down the valley past the two Wallabarrow farms to join the road at Dunnerdale Bridge where the main road crosses the river. There is a useful bus service between Seathwaite, Ulpha Bridge, Broughton and Ulverston, with connections at Duddon Bridge for Millom. If you are walking you can avoid the main road by following a bridle track signposted 'High Kiln Bank' (a Youth Hostel): this track joins the road again near Ulpha Bridge.

The Sepulchre

The next place of interest down the valley is Ulpha; opposite the Travellers' Rest Inn, on the far side of the river, is a square enclosure with firs, known as The Sepulchre; it was the burying ground of an old Quaker family who lived at Woodend.

The very attractive Ulpha Church is a short distance below the

inn, and from the churchyard is a fine view of the river. Below
this point the main road crosses the river again, and the pedestrian
has the choice of two routes. The cyclist or motorist will cross the
bridge and follow the road down a charming valley, joining the
main road at Duddon Bridge, a mile before reaching the small market
town of Broughton-in-Furness.

The Lady's Dub

If the pedestrian is following the valley towards the foot, a better
plan is to keep to the right of the river for a half-mile until an old
mill is reached by the side of Holehouse Ghyll, a charming ravine
worth exploring for a short distance as far as the waterfall known as
the Lady's Dub, where tradition has it that Lady Ulpha was worried
by a wolf.

Just above the mill a road branches to the left, dropping down
the left of the ghyll and, soon after, a second track forks to the left
through a gate close by the ghyll. This is the track to follow, but it
is of interest to note that half a mile down the first road is an old
farmhouse called Frith Hall, said to have been built as a hunting lodge.
It later became an inn where, in 1730, seventeen couples were
married by the local minister.

Ulpha Park

The track from the mill enters a wood, much of which was cut
down during the last war, passes close by the river for a few yards
and continues through Ulpha Park, rising up at Beckfoot to join
the road which leads by Duddon Hall to Duddon Bridge, where the
main road from Millom can be followed over the bridge to Broughton,
one and a half miles further.

Broughton-in-Furness, so called to distinguish it from Broughton
East at the foot of Windermere, is a small market town pleasantly
situated near the mouth of the Duddon. A stone obelisk has been
erected in the centre of the market square to the memory of John
Gilpin, who gave the site to the town. There are also some old
stocks. There is a fine Norman doorway on the south side of the
church which, built in the Early English style, is dedicated to St.
Mary Magdalene.

AROUND THE DUDDON VALLEY

Being a short deep valley, it falls about 2,000 feet in its fourteen
miles between the Three Shire Stone and Broughton; there are not
many walks of the easy class, but there are several interesting fell
climbs. One of the interesting easy walks which requires few
directions is to follow the road up one side of the river from

Duddon Bridge to Seathwaite and return from Hall Dunnerdale down
the other side, the return distance between Broughton and Seathwaite
being sixteen miles, with little climbing.

From Ulpha, Hall Dunnerdale, Seathwaite, Birks Bridge, Cockley
Beck and the Duddon Bridge, it is possible to make interesting walks
between any of the named places, using both sides of the river.

The following routes are all in either the moderate or strenuous
class.

Route 91. Follow the main road from Broughton towards Coniston
for a mile and a half to Lower Hawthwaite, then along a narrow
secondary road on the left signposted 'Broughton Mills'. Cross
the River Lickle below the mill, and turn right immediately over
the bridge to follow a fell road which leads along the side of Stickle
Pike to Far Kiln Bank, where you turn left to join the main road at
the bridge below Ulpha Church. Continue down this road for a mile
until you reach a point where the road nears the river. A rough
track will be seen starting on the left side of the road which rises
through a break in the hillside. Follow this track over the rise to
join another narrow road coming up the valley on the other side.
A short distance along this, then fork right to follow a lane past
Hawes, Croglinhurst to Lower Bleansley, where you turn left by
Low Moss to cross the Lickle and then on to the main road leading
back to Broughton. A delightful ramble through interesting country.
11 miles. (Moderate.)

Route 92. From Broughton, take the path from the Square through
Tower Park and cross the railway, then through fields and along a
lane, turn right, through a farmyard and on to the Low Road from
Coniston. Turn left, and, just before reaching a five-arched railway
bridge, take the lane on the right, through two fields and a wood to
Rosethwaite Farm. At the junction of the road from the disused
Woodland station, turn right downhill.

Take the first lane on the left after crossing the stream, through
Bridge End Farm, and follow the stream to some cottages where the
road ends. Keep to the right bank for the next two miles until a
wood is reached, when the beck is left for a scramble up the fell side.
Climb over the fence and continue to follow the beck until the old
road to Coniston is met. Turn left and, after crossing the old railway
track, turn right on to the main road.

Just before reaching Torver station, turn up a lane on the left at
some cottages, which leads on to open fell and to a small quarry.
Then strike left for a solitary tree on the fell side. A path now leads
to some quarries. Avoid all quarry roads and follow the left bank
of the Appletree Worth Beck, past an old house overlooking the

gorge; cross the beck by the stepping stones and at the junction of
the Walna Scar track turn left over the bridge and continue along
this road until it joins the main road back to Broughton. *14 miles.
(Moderate.)*

Route 93. WALNA SCAR. This walk can start at Broughton,
in which case follow Route 89 to Broughton Mills, then turn right
instead of crossing the river and fork left a mile and a half along this
road to cross Appletree Worth Beck near Stock Beck. Three miles
of road walking can be saved by taking the bus to Woodland. From
the old station take the road leading uphill, turn left along the main
Broughton—Coniston road for a few yards, then turn right along the
first lane, go through a gate and over the hill, turn right along the
next lane to cross the bridge over Appletree Worth Beck. You have
now joined the route from Broughton and this proceeds up the
small but charming Lickle Valley. The rise is gradual and, higher up,
our track crosses the river, now a small beck, to join a track coming up
the other side from Stephenson Ground.

Leaving the valley, it reaches open fell land, and the track in parts is
difficult to follow. There is a grand view to the left of the upper
Duddon Valley, with Harter Fell, the Scafell and Bowfell group of
fells in the background. Continue along the fell side until the track
joins the Walna Scar Pass. If desired, you can drop down the pass
to Seathwaite and return down the Duddon Valley to Broughton.
If not, then follow the pass to its summit. Here another alternative
route is possible. If desired, to shorten the walk, continue by the
pass down the other side and at the first bridge either fork right for
Woodland or left for Coniston; the former is two and a half miles
from the top of the pass and to Coniston is three miles.

If time and energy permit, it is worth while doing some of the
peaks from the top of Walna Scar Pass. A short sharp climb due
north leads to the top of Brown Pike, and then follows an easy ridge
walk on to Dow Crag where there is some excellent rock scenery;
at the bottom lies Goats Water and opposite, behind Goats Water,
is Coniston Old Man.

To reach the Old Man, continue north of Dow Crag, then bear
right into a big hollow where there is a welcome spring, and then
follows a short rise to the summit of Coniston Old Man.

The view has been described in the Coniston section, as has the
route of the descent to Coniston to join the bus back to Broughton.
12 miles from Woodland to Coniston. (Strenuous.)

Route 94. ESKDALE. Proceed to Seathwaite. Continue up the
valley to Birks Bridge. There is a route up either side of the river
from here. The right-hand route goes to Cockley Beck, then crosses
the bridge and follows a rough fell road over Hard Knott Pass. By

Fell Hounds   Coniston

Sawrey   Beatrix Potter's Home

Braithwaite   High Bridge

Grasmere Sports   Cumberland Wrestling

crossing Birks Bridge, another track goes to the left of the river by Black Hall, joining Hard Knott Pass shortly after. Follow the pass over into Eskdale and note the Hard Knott Fort halfway down on the right-hand side. Reaching the valley, continue down the road to the first bridge, Wha House Bridge, or by path described in Route 97. There is a pleasant walk down the left side of the river from here through the fields by Penny Hill, and this can be followed as far as Stanley Ghyll.

Immediately after crossing a wooden footbridge over the beck, which flows down Stanley Ghyll, turn left to follow a path up to the right of the stream. A mile up this ghyll is Dalegarth Force a fine waterfall, and a path to the right, just before reaching the third bridge across the river, leads up the cliff side to overlook the falls. This path crosses a stile, joins a road which can be followed over Birker Moor to Ulpha, catching the bus at Ulpha Bridge back to Broughton, or wherever you may be staying in the Duddon Valley. *Seathwaite to Ulpha by Eskdale, 15 miles. (Moderate.)*

Note. There is a shorter route back from the Eskdale side of Hard Knott Pass. It starts at the cattle grid near the foot of the pass, crosses the beck, and, bearing left, rises round the side of Harter Fell and in just over a mile it begins a long gradual descent of Grassguards The objection to this route is that you miss much of the beauties of Eskdale encountered between Hard Knott and Stanley Ghyll, and the land around Grassguards is very boggy, especially after rain.

Route 95. BOWFELL. Proceed up the Duddon Valley, past Cockley Beck, and to the Three Shire Stone at the head of Wrynose. Follow Route 56 over Crinkle Crags to Bowfell.

The shortest return to the Duddon is by the same route, but if an alternative route is desired, return to the Three Tarns between Bowfell and Crinkle Crags, then drop down the fell side towards Eskdale, keeping to the left of Lincove Beck. There is no proper path at first, but one appears lower down. Continue down the valley past Esk Falls Bridge to Brotherilkeld, keeping the river on your right all the way.

A short distance past the farm at Brotherilkeld, turn left to climb over Hard Knott Pass to Cockley Beck at the other side. Although the distance round from Cockley Beck is only thirteen miles it is a fairly strenuous ramble and should not be attempted when the tops are cloud-covered. *(Strenuous.)*

Route 96. CARRS. Follow Route 95 to the top of Wrynose, then turn right instead of left at the Three Shire Stone. There is a short but steep climb up on to Wet Side Edge, but once the ridge is reached it is quite easy going. Follow the ridge which rises in a southerly direction to the top of Carrs.

G

Bear right from here to the summit of Grey Friar, only a short distance away from which is an excellent view of the Duddon Valley with Black Combe in the background. Return to Carrs, or make your way round the side of Swirl How on to Great How Crags. From Carrs, cross over to Swirl How, then follow an easy, pleasant ridge walk over Great How Crags, Fairfield and Brim Fell on to Coniston Old Man. There is a good footpath all the way so no difficulty with the route should be experienced.

From the Old Man drop to Goats Water, and a footpath follows the course of the beck down to join the Walna Scar Pass. Proceed up the pass and down the other side to Seathwaite. *The complete round is 15 miles. (Strenuous.)*

Route 97. BLACK COMBE. Start from Broughton, or the Duddon Bridge. There is a footpath which starts near the bridge behind some houses, it climbs up through a wood and winds round the countryside thick with bracken. It crosses a road and continues over a valley to cross a second road. At this point it is advisable to turn left down the road as far as Crag Hall, then right up to the Stone Circle.

The path referred to above is not easy to find and, although delightful in dry weather, should be avoided after rain. A slightly longer and less interesting route, but one that is easier to find, is to follow the main road from Duddon Bridge down the valley towards Millom and take the second by-road to the right which is the old main road over the fells to Bootle. Fork left at Crag Hall to the Stone Circle. This fine circle stands in a field on the right and can be seen from some distance away.

Continue to Swinside Farm near the Circle. Behind the farm a track starts in a westerly direction. Keep right when the path forks up the right side of a short wide valley. There is a footpath to the top near where the stream has its source. Next follows a long rough ridge walk, keeping to the left of the fence, heading for the top of Black Combe which can be seen in the west. Be careful not to take the track which crosses the ridge and drops to the right of the summit to Bootle; near the final rise, bear slightly left.

Black Combe is not an attractive fell but this is compensated for by the grand view from the summit which, on a clear day, includes the Scottish, Irish and Welsh coasts, the Isle of Man, Morecambe Bay and Blackpool Tower, the Furness, Lancashire and Yorkshire fells and many of the principal Lakeland peaks. It was used as a look-out station during the war and there is a good track on the coast side dropping to the start of the Whitcham Valley near Silecroft. The bus to Millom stops at the road end, and at Millom the Cumberland bus connects with the Ribble for Broughton and Ulverston. *8 miles. (Moderate.)*

ESKDALE

IT IS A GREAT PITY THAT ESKDALE is so difficult to reach, for it is one of the most interesting and charming valleys in the Lake District. The best approach in the summer months is by train from Ravenglass. From opposite the main line station, a miniature train starts for Eskdale. It is run by the Ravenglass and Eskdale Railway Company and is of fifteen-inch gauge, with open and covered-in carriages pulled by a steam engine, the exact model of the large engines, or by a diesel oil engine. The seven miles to the other terminus at Eskdale is through beautiful scenery all the way.

The River Esk rises high on Esk Hause and flows beneath Scafell Pike and Esk Pike, with tributaries joining it off Scafell and Bowfell, so that by the time it reaches Brotherilkeld at the foot of Hard Knott t is quite a wide river. From Esk Falls Bridge to Wha House Bridge it is full of charming pools and cascades, then the attractive river passes through scenery consisting of craggy fell side and charming woodlands until it reaches the estuary at Eskmeals. The Esk is one of the rivers which can be followed almost its entire length from source to sea, and it is beautiful all the way.

As previously stated, most Lakeland valleys are best approached from the foot, and Eskdale is no exception.

Ravenglass

Ravenglass lies at the foot of the valley on the big estuary formed by the meeting of the Rivers Esk, Mite and Irt. In the days of the Romans it was an important seaport, but the harbour, large and well protected in those days, has since been silted up, although as recently as the last century boats sailed from here to the Isle of Man, and it was a favourite haunt for smugglers. The village consists of a single street alongside the estuary, and a market charter was granted to it in 1209, but no market is ever held there now.

Across the estuary on the line of sand dunes is a protected gullery where thousands of birds, including the rare terns, nest and breed. Application to visit it may be made to the County Council.

Walls Castle

Crossing the footbridge from the station away from the village, a footpath leads to a private carriage drive to which the public are admitted. A short distance along here on the left is a ruined building which is all that remains of Walls Castle, the bath-house of a Roman fort which used to stand close by. There the visitor can see the pink cement that decorated the interior and the empty niche which once held the statue of the Goddess of Fortune, for the bath-house was the clubroom of the Roman soldiers, and any who wished to implore her help before gambling could do so.

Continuing along the drive, through beautifully wooded avenues, private house and lodge are passed on the right and a little farther on the route goes through the farmyard of Newtown. Passing through a gate beyond, the visitor should turn left up the slopes to the top of the fell in front. Here are the remains of Newtown Knott Beacon Tower, erected in 1823 as a guide to ships entering Ravenglass Harbour. Until it collapsed a few years ago it was regularly white-washed to make it clearly visible to ships at sea. In Roman days this point was a look-out post and signal station for the garrison of the fort commanding the harbour below. The view is one of the finest which can be reached in about half an hour from Ravenglass station.

The Gates of Paradise

Another attraction near Ravenglass is Muncaster Castle. The entrance is about a mile up the main road from Ravenglass, and the grounds are open to the public from Easter to 30 September, from 1 to 6 p.m. daily at a small charge. The grounds, which should be visited in May and June to be seen at their best, are full of ornamental bushes including rhododendrons and azaleas, and the beautiful terrace walk, starting from the front of the castle, was likened by Ruskin to 'The Gates of Paradise'.

The castle, which is also open on certain days, grew up round a fourteenth-century peel tower, which is now incorporated in the present building at the south-west aspects and is known as Agricola's Tower. The site may have originally been a Roman look-out station, for a gold coin of the Roman Emperor, Theodosius the Great, A.D. 375, was unearthed in the foundations of the tower during recon-struction operations about 140 years ago.

Muncaster Church, near the back entrance of the castle, is of considerable antiquity. The present building, much restored, is of the fifteenth century, but stands on an older foundation. Its date is unknown, but there are records going back to 1190. There are interesting old brasses in the chancel, and a rood window high in the south wall of the nave. In the churchyard are two fragments of Viking crosses and two old yews.

Those desiring to approach Eskdale on foot should proceed along the road a short distance beyond the entrance to the castle grounds, then, at a point where the main road turns sharp right at the top of a short hill, keep ahead in the same direction up a long straight lane. This rises for some distance before passing through a gate on to open fell.

The Luck of Muncaster

A short distance to the right from this gate is a slender tower of light-coloured stone known as Chapels. It was built by Lord Muncaster at the end of the eighteenth century to commemorate the meeting place between Henry VI and a shepherd after his defeat at the battle of Towton. The King had been wandering over the fells after being refused sanctuary at Irton Hall. He was taken by the shepherd to the Lord of Muncaster, Sir John Pennington, and in gratitude for the hospitality received the King presented to his host a shallow bowl or chalice of greenish glass ornamented with dots of gold and enamel. It is still preserved by the family, and known as the 'Luck of Muncaster', for so long as it remains there no bad luck will befall the house. It is used at baptisms of members of the Pennington family.

A forest road rises to the left, passing a small lake partly hidden by rhododendron bushes on the left. At a gate beyond the tarn a footpath starts and winds round to the right of Hooker Crag, the foremost peak, and it is worth a slight diversion to climb to the top of this peak for the excellent view.

Muncaster Head

The pony-track continues along the fell side, and is quite easy to follow. It passes a flat rock bearing the name 'Ross's Camp, 1882', which was once a popular picnicking spot for the people from Muncaster Castle. Farther on, the track passes through a gate and descends with an excellent view of Eskdale in front. At the bottom the path winds to the right, crosses a small beck and climbs to the right of the next hill, then drops to pass through a gate; the track down to the gate is often very wet underfoot, and boots are essential. Continue along the path, following the waymarks, to join a rough farm road at a point where there is a gate across it. Pass through another nearby gate on the left as you face Muncaster Head and follow the path through a field, turn right into a second field, keep left to a third field, followed by a narrow lane which passes Eskdale Green station to join the main road. Turn right, and follow the road past the King George IV Hotel to a $\frac{1}{4}$ mile along the Ulpha road. Immediately over Forge Ho Bridge which spans the River Esk, turn left and continue along waymarked track by the riverside about a mile. The scenery is very pretty. The track leaves the river by a big pool and passes through a plantation containing a great variety of old and new trees. Bear right at the fork, to emerge on to a green close to Dalegarth Hall.

Dalegarth Hall

This building is easily recognized by its strange massive round chimneys, which were typical of the district in the fifteenth century when it was built. Now a farm, it formed part of a mansion which was pulled down about 1750, the dining-room had an elaborate ornamental plaster ceiling and bore the date 1599 with the initials E. S. A., those of the then owner and his wife, Edward and Anne

Stanley. The original building dates back to 1181.

Proceeding along the common, pass through the second gate on the left to enter a wood. A Planning Board notice near gate is an indication of right gate. Follow a footpath which quickly leads to the side of a stream and proceeds up its banks. This is Stanley Ghyll, one of the prettiest ghylls in the Lake District. For the next mile it is bounded on each side by precipitous crags which are greatly enhanced by the variety of exquisitely fresh and luxuriant ferns which adorn them from head to foot. Near the top the beck is crossed three times by wooden footbridges, and above the last is a fine waterfall of 60 feet known as Dalegarth Force.

Boot

Returning over the top bridge, a footpath strikes up the cliff side on the left, and by following this, keeping left all the way, it will lead to the top of the cliff where you can look down on the falls from above. There is a fine view of Boot with Scafell in the background. The path now crosses a stone wall and joins a road down which you descend until you return to Dalegarth Hall. Continue along the road, crossing Trough House Bridge (note the flood marks on the bridge) to join another road beside the War Memorial and school. Turn right, and half a mile up the road, past Eskdale station, the terminus of the Ravenglass and Eskdale Railway, is a crossroads, and by turning left you will reach the village of Boot where there is an interesting old mill open to the public in summer.

There is a charming beck walk from the post office. Turn through a gate on the right before crossing the bridge, and for the next half-mile the Whillan Beck is a continual series of charming cascades. Leave the road at the first gate and have a look at the beck and the pretty falls. Return to the road and follow this up the hill to Gill Bank. A short distance above the mill is Buckpot Falls, the hole into which the water falls is the deepest in Lakeland.

Tommy Dobson

From the crossroads near Boot is another interesting walk; instead of turning left for the village, turn right and soon the track brings you to St. Catherine's Church. In the churchyard can be seen the grave of Tommy Dobson, whom many consider to have been an even finer huntsman than the more famous John Peel. The next mile along the river is also of great charm, and finally we arrive at Doctor's Bridge, so called because, about 1740, it was widened to allow the doctor's gig to pass over. The structure of the original bridge can still be seen beneath the present one. A little farther on the track joins the main road close by the Woolpack Inn, and just beyond is the Youth Hostel.

By crossing the Doctor's Bridge, you can visit Birker Force, a fine fall of 60 feet, or follow the track beyond Penny Hill on to Harter Fell. Another delightful walk is to cross the bridge and return down the other side of the river to the foot of Stanley Ghyll and Dalegarth Hall.

Brotherilkeld

Continuing up the valley past the Woolpack Inn, another mile brings the visitor to the foot of Hard Knott Pass. A short distance up the valley, beyond the foot of the pass, is an ancient farmhouse called Brotherilkeld or Butterilket, one of the few Lakeland farms with a history which has come down to us. Its original name was Norse, meaning 'the Booths of Olfkil', and it was colonized by the early Norse immigrants, who settled in pre-Norman Cumberland. In 1210, it was granted by Alan de Pennington, Lord of Muncaster, to his brother David. In 1242 David exchanged it with monks of Furness Abbey for Monk Foss, near Bootle. The monks used it as a grazing ground until the Dissolution of the monasteries, when it came into the possession of the Stanley family. It is now the property of the Forestry Commission.

Hard Knott Castle

About a third of the way up Hard Knott Pass, a hundred yards to the left of the road, is a quadrangular enclosure of stones marking the site of a Roman fort known as Hard Knott Castle. This fort is almost square, with corners rounded and towers at each facing the four points of the compass. It measures on the outer face 375 feet on each side. In Roman days there was an earthen rampart to which the thick walls formed a revetment. The four gateways may still be traced, one midway between each tower. The gate at the south-west, facing the summit of the pass, was the Pretorian Gate. The north-east gate has a road passing from it for about 210 yards to a well-engineered, artificially cleared and levelled piece of ground of nearly three acres, the Roman parade ground. On the north-west side of the parade ground is a raised mound approached by a ramp which was the grandstand of the commanding officers.

Inside the fort, three buildings have left their remains. That next to the north-east gate was a granary and storehouse. In the centre was the headquarters building, about 70 feet square, having a court-yard in front and business offices at the back. The third building lies to the south-west of the headquarters and was the commanding officer's quarters.

Outside the fort, between the Pretorian gateway and the present road, is the Roman bath-house, which consisted of two separate buildings, one a block of three rooms with heating furnace and cold and tepid baths, the other was a circular building approached by a ramp which was the sweating room for the baths, and its roof would

have been of bronze, with louvres to regulate the heat. Its interior
had been cemented with the usual pink cement found in Roman
bath-houses and other buildings. This site has recently been
excavated by the Department of the Environment.

AROUND ESKDALE

Some of the easier walks have already been described, others are
detailed below and also a number of strenuous walks. By walking
over Hard Knott Pass to Cockley Beck, some of the walks described
in the Duddon section can be included.

Route 98. EEL TARN. Start from Boot post office and turn in
through the first gate on the right, immediately preceding the bridge,
and walk along the farm track on the right side of the Whillan Beck.
Near the top of the hill, pass through a gate on the right, turn left,
and keep to the track on the right side of the stone wall. Soon this
track passes through a gate on to open fell land.

Continue in an easterly direction to Eel Tarn, passing to the left
of the tarn, crossing at right angles a footpath, marked by white
crosses, from Burnmoor to the Woolpack. Continue east to Stony
Tarn, passing this to the left, then make for the left of a small hillock
which overlooks the tarn to the east, and drop down the slope to the
left on the other side. Cross Cowcove Beck, then bear right, dropping
down in the direction of the stream until a shepherd's track is
reached which winds down to the valley and crosses Cowcove Beck
in the bottom below some fine falls. The track leads down the valley
past Taw House to join the main road back to Boot. *7 miles. (Easy.)*

Route 99. CAM SPOUT. Follow the road from Boot up the
valley, leaving it before crossing the river at Wha House Bridge to
take the track on the left over Cowcove Beck, and up the fell side
by the winding path which is the reverse of the previous route from
Cowcove Beck. At the top of the rise the wide track narrows to
a footpath, and winds round the foot of High Scarth Crag in a
north-easterly direction for two miles to Cam Spout Falls. The falls
are above the point where the path crosses the river, and from here
the path rises sharply between Scafell and Scafell Pike on to
Mickledore. That, however, is for a strenuous walk described later.

For this easy to moderate walk, return from the falls along a path
which forks to the left, and crossing the beck, which is actually the
beginning of the River Esk, drops down to the left of it to a pack-
horse bridge in the valley at the junction of the Rivers Esk and
Lingcove. Above the bridge are the Throstlegarth Falls, two fine
falls of about 25 feet each, the lower being in a very pretty setting.

Crossing the bridge, there is a good footpath down the valley. The
river on the right has many charming cascades, until it reaches the
farm at Brotherilkeld where the road starts which leads back to Boot.
12 miles. The road can be avoided by walking up Hard Knott Pass
to the cattle grid. Across this, turn right. cross the stream by the bridge,
and, about 50 yards along the pony track, turn off to the right along a
footpath near the wall. This leads to a stile; follow the path from
here to Penny Hill Farm, after crossing Doctor's Bridge over the Esk,
turn left and follow the riverside track down to St. Catherine's
Church, then along the farm road to Boot, a delightful walk.

Route 100. DEVOKE WATER. Start at the old schoolhouse
below Dalegarth station, along the road over the river to Dalegarth
Hall. The road rises shortly after passing the Hall, and continues to
do so more or less through Low Ground and High Ground Farms until
it reaches a crossroads. A diversion can be made by visiting Stanley
Ghyll as already described. Cross right over the road and continue
along a rough fell road to Devoke Water. There is nothing very
attractive about this lake, which is the reservoir for Millom. Keep
along the fell side on the right of the lake, about fifty yards or more
from the water to avoid the wet ground, until you reach the head,
drop down to cross the beck a short distance below where it leaves
the lake, and a footpath can be followed down to the left of Linbeck
Ghyll to join the road in the valley. Turn right at the farm and follow
the road back to the George IV Hotel. The station is a quarter mile
beyond the hotel and you can return to Boot by the train.
If walking to Boot, it is a better plan to follow the right bank of
the river from Forge House Bridge to Dalegarth Hall. *Boot to Eskdale
Green Station, 7 miles. (Moderate.)*

Route 101. MITERDALE. This can be called the Hidden Valley,
for Miterdale is one of the least-known valleys in the Lake District.
The starting point for this walk is Eskdale Green post office, best
reached from Boot by train to Eskdale Green station, then walking up
the hill from the station. A few yards beyond the post office in the
direction of Boot, the main road turns sharp right while at the same
time a narrow lane begins to rise from the corner on the left. It passes
Gate House, a fine mansion, with some fine wooded grounds
including a moderately sized artificial lake. The building is now used
as an Outward Bound school.
At the top of the rise the road turns left, passes a farm, Low Holme,
joins another road coming up from Irton Road, turns right and
soon after crosses the River Mite. The road continues up the valley
to a farm building. Pass through the yard and then cross the river on
your right by a bridge, continue right up the valley in front to reach
some crags. There is a short, sharp climb at the top to Burnmoor

Tarn. Bear right, past the gamekeeper's cottage until the Burnmoor pony-track is reached, then follow this back to Boot. *7 miles. (Moderate.)*

Route 102. THE SCREES. Follow the previous route to the point where the road from Irton Road joins it, cross the stile and then the river, and continue along the path up through the plantation which rises at an easy gradient until it crosses a stone stile at the top. It is possible to follow the path down the other side into Wasdale, but for the purpose of this walk turn right and keep by the wall, then, when it ends, make for the foremost peak, which is Whin Rigg. By stepping a few yards towards the lake, some of the fine crags of the Screes overlooking Wastwater can be seen. The lake itself lies deep below and great care must be exercised because of the crags.

From the summit drop towards the next peak, Illgill Head, and for the next mile the path goes along the top of the Screes, skirting the crags on the left through which glimpses of the lake can frequently be seen. From the top of Illgill Head is a fine view embracing Wasdale Head, Gable, Scafell, Yewbarrow and Buckbarrow, Harter Fell, the Coniston Fells and Crinkle Crags. The path continues in the direction of Wasdale Head for a short distance, then, as it begins to drop and Burnmoor Tarn appears below, strike off to the right in the direction of the tarn, joining the pony-track to the left of it and then by the track back to Boot. *10 miles. (Fairly strenuous.)* For Wasdale Head keep left from Illgill Head, right of a stone wall, and a path leads down to the Burnmoor Track and Wasdale Head.

Route 103. HARTER FELL. Proceed up the valley to the Woolpack Inn. A few yards to the Boot side of the inn go down a lane on the right, crossing the river a short distance beyond by Doctor's Bridge. Follow the lane to the next farm at Penny Hill then, having passed the farm, turn right up the second track which quickly becomes a footpath, rugged and steep as it ascends, crosses a fell beck and then joins the track coming in from Brotherilkeld. From here the path is difficult to follow and the best plan is to head for the summit of the fell which can be seen in the distance. There is some good scrambling near the top but avoid the crags on the northern slope.

The view includes the Scafell group to the north and the Coniston Fells to the south-east, there is also a good view of the Eskdale and Duddon valleys. Continue in a north to north-east direction towards Bowfell, the ground is rather broken in parts and care is needed, but after the first sharp drop the gradient is quite easy until it reaches Hard Knott Pass. Turn left down the pass to the valley which leads down to Boot. *6½ miles (Fairly strenuous.)*

Route 104. SCAFELL. Follow Route 99 to Cam Spout. After crossing the beck the path rises sharply to the right of the falls and gradually the mighty crags close in on both sides. The path reaches some rough scree at the bottom of Mickledore and at a point where the beck coming down from Foxes Tarn is passed on the left, leave the main track to follow a path up between the crags on the left until a pool named Foxes Tarn is reached. Not far above this is the top of Scafell.

A more exciting route, but one that needs care, and should not be attempted in bad or uncertain weather, is to continue up the scree route to the top of Mickledore, a narrow ridge which separates Scafell from Scafell Pike.

To reach the summit of Scafell Pike, the highest English mountain, is a simple matter from here. Cross the ridge to the east and a footpath rises over rough ground and in about twenty minutes the summit of the Pike is reached. The view includes Windermere, Derwentwater and Wastwater Lakes, Scafell with its rugged crags lies close at hand and to the north is another mighty fell, Great Gable. Many other prominent peaks are visible, too many to mention here.

A good circular route is to descend from the Pike in an easterly direction by the well-marked footpath which crosses rocky ground in the direction of Great End, then swings to the right of this fell to descend to Esk Hause. A footpath from the signpost passes the shelter and drops down the valley between Scafell Pike and Esk Pike, by the beck which is the start of the River Esk; this leads to Cam Spout, and you can either return by the route of your ascent from Cowcove Beck or by Esk Falls, as described in Route 99.

For Scafell, which is slightly lower than the Pike, the route from Mickledore is to hug the rock face and descend by a track to Lord's Rake and ascend as described in Route 27.

The best descent from Scafell is in the direction of Wastwater, swinging round lower down to Burnmoor Tarn, then follow the pony-track back to Boot. Another is over Slight Side to Boot.

This is one of the routes where it is inadvisable to give the distance, but the climb should take the average person $3\frac{1}{2}$ hours, Scafell by Lord's Rake at least half an hour longer, and the return from Scafell 2 hours, from Scafell Pike $2\frac{1}{2}$ hours.

Route 105. BOWFELL. Proceed up the valley and over Hard Knott Pass to Cockley Beck, then up Wrynose to the Three Shire Stone. Now follow the footpath on the left up Cold Pike on to Crinkle Crags and Bowfell (see Route 56).

To return to Eskdale, retrace the last part of the route between Bowfell and the Three Tarns and at the latter turn right in the direction of Eskdale. The path is difficult to follow at first, but simply keep going down towards the valley and keep to the left of Lingcove Beck.

which is formed by the meeting of three becks in Green Hole.
Lower down a good footpath appears which leads down to Esk
Falls Bridge, then down the valley to Boot. This is a grand ramble,
embracing some fine rock scenery, but is very strenuous. *(16 miles.)*

WASDALE

WASDALE IS UNLIKE ANY OTHER VALLEY in the Lake District, and
the only lake in Britain bearing any resemblance to Wastwater is
Loch Awe in Scotland. It has a wild and majestic appearance. Many
who first visit Wasdale, especially if it is a dull day, consider that it is a
dull, gloomy, depressing lake; but there is something strange about
Wasdale, the more you visit it the more it draws like a huge magnet
until, to many, it has become the most attractive valley here.

Many consider there is no finer view anywhere than that from the
side of Wastwater looking towards the head of the valley where the
Screes tower majestically above on the right, rising almost
perpendicularly from the black-looking water, its darkness significant
of its depth. On a calm day the water reflects every detail of the
Screes like a huge mirror. In the background is that fine group of
fells which includes Scafell, Lingmell, Gable, Yewbarrow, and Red
Pike.

Wasdale is difficult to reach. Gosforth, ten miles from the Head,
is the nearest point on a regular bus service. There is an infrequent
bus service on Thursdays and Saturdays to Netherwasdale, six miles
from the Head. Beyond the village the only means of approach is by
car, cycle or on foot. The nearest other approach on foot is from
Seatoller, a distance of six miles over Sty Head Pass, which, although
rough, is not strenuous.

Gosforth is the nearest village and its church is of interest to the
visitor for it contains some very old Chinese bells and stone coffins.
In the churchyard is a fourteen feet high cross of Viking age, its
carvings showing a confusion of the Christian and pagan religions.

The church at Netherwasdale (or Strand), the village for Wasdale
four miles from Gosforth, is also of interest. The next six miles to
Wasdale Head is rather more interesting as the road travels the full
length of Wastwater.

Wasdale Head, a small hamlet of one hotel, several farms and
a church, used to boast of four things: the deepest lake, the highest
mountain, the smallest church and the biggest liar. The latter,
Will Ritson, a well-known 'character' of the nineteenth century,
was said to be able to beat any tall story that could be told. A service
is held in the small church on Sunday afternoons, and in the
churchyard are the graves of several who lost their lives scaling the
great rocks on Gable and Scafell.

AROUND WASDALE

Route 106. THE SCREES. The start of this walk is the village
of Netherwasdale. Leave the village in the direction of the Screes
and soon you arrive at a road junction formed like a triangle with a
rough grass and rocky centre. Turn right towards Santon Bridge
and cross the river at the right corner of the triangle. If approaching
this from the lake you keep left at the triangle to cross the river.
Immediately over the river is a stile on the left and a bridle track on
the other side leads through a field and a plantation, then rises up the
side of Irton Pike which is the fell in front. On arriving at the top
of the climb at a stone wall turn left and keep to the left of the wall up
to the top of Whin Rigg.

An alternative route from the bridge is to cross the stile and follow
the bridle road for a quarter mile, then bear left following the side of
the wall until you pass Easthwaite Farm. The path continues along
the foot of the fell until you reach a stile. A path from here goes up
through the narrow gorge of Greathall Gill. If approaching this
route from the lake, start from a stone stile on your left where the road
leaves the lake to go up to a cattle grid. The track follows the shore
for over a mile, past the end of the lake, down the river side for a
short distance before crossing it by Lund Bridge, then by a footpath
to the foot of the lake. Just before reaching the lake, a footpath
commences on the right and rises sharply up the fell side by Greathall
Gill through a gully near the top between the crags, until it joins
the path from Irton Pike near to the summit of Whin Rigg.

The rest of the route along the Screes is described in Route 102.
9 miles

Route 107. RED PIKE, PILLAR. This climb starts from Overbeck,
the second of the two rivers which flow into Wastwater on the
roadside approaching it from the foot of the lake. The path rises
to the right of the beck, which has many pretty cascades; after about
a half-mile it crosses the beck and continues up the other side. Higher
up, the climber is faced by the side of Red Pike and can either bear
right on to Dore Head and climb the ridge of Red Pike or bear left to
climb up the side towards the cairn which can be seen near the top.
Low Tarn lies below on the left.

The last part to the cairn entails some good scrambling over the
rocks. The cairn itself is not the actual summit, but is the better
viewpoint. The actual summit is a short distance beyond. The
route now lies along a wide grassy ridge with deep crags on either
side, the path is easy to follow as later it swings to the right, passing
below the summit of Steeple which is to the left. It drops suddenly,
crosses a narrow gap named Wind Gap and then there is a short
but steep climb up the far side on to the summit of Pillar Mountain.

The most famous portion of the Pillar is the huge rock which juts out on the Ennerdale side known as the Pillar Rock or Nose. It is only accessible to climbers with ropes and should not be attempted by the ordinary walker. A footpath enabling the visitor to obtain a close-up view of this massive rock starts on the Ennerdale side of the summit cairn and drops down to the rock. The main climbs are round the other side and cannot be seen from this point.

From the fell summit a wire fence is a good guide, although the path is easy to follow as it continues along the top of the fell towards Gable. After a while the path drops sharply by some big rocks and forks at the bottom. The left-hand track is easy to follow on to Looking Stead, but the right fork, which is the one to take for Wasdale, is not so clear and it is best to make down the fell side towards the valley. Lower down, the path will be picked up and this crosses to the far side of the valley to join the pony-track coming down Black Sail Pass. Follow this down to Wasdale Head. *The circular route is 10 miles, taking five to six hours.*

Route 108. SCAFELL PIKE. 3,210 feet. The ascent of this fell from several centres has already been described. Wasdale Head is one of the best starting points and there are several routes.

One is by Lingmell, Brown Tongue and Hollow Stones, but it is a tedious climb and preferable as a return route.

A second, and probably the best known, is to climb Sty Head Pass, then on to Esk Hause, or by the Guides Route: both these routes are described in Route 104.

A more interesting route is by the Piers Ghyll track. Start from Wasdale Head in the direction of Sty Head Pass, and at the point where the pass begins to rise sharply a footpath branches to the right, which should be followed to the point where Lingmell Beck joins the beck from Piers Ghyll. Cross just above the junction and follow the left side of Piers Beck. Cross the beck again immediately above the fork with Greta Ghyll and keep left of Piers Ghyll. This ghyll is very dangerous and the walker should not attempt to go into the ghyll itself, but should keep to the left. Higher up there is a scramble up some rocks, then along a steep grassy slope joining the Guides Route at the top. On no account should it be attempted on the *right* side of the ghyll and should be avoided altogether in bad weather.

A safer route from the junction of the two streams at the foot of Piers Ghyll is to follow a footpath between the two becks, rather nearer Lingmell Beck on the left. Higher up, the path swings to the left towards the top of Sty Head Pass, then it is time to leave the path and climb up the fell side on the right towards a big boulder; just above the boulder the Guides Route is reached, turn right along here, over Greta Ghyll, following the route to Scafell Pike as already described.

There are several routes by which you can return to Wasdale Head, one by Esk Hause and Sty Head, which is the longest. It starts in an easterly direction from the summit cairn to the left of the shelter, then continues east towards Great End, swinging to the right of Long Pike on the Esk Hause, then down by Sprinkling Tarn and Sty Head Pass.

A second is to start opposite the Memorial Tablet on the cairn in the direction of Wastwater, fork right at the junction about 80 yards from the summit, towards Lingmell. When clear of the crags the path swings left towards Wastwater again and soon the rocks disappear and there is a grassy footpath on to Brown Tongue. A long drop down the middle of the Tongue leads to a beck which is crossed and the footpath winds round the side of Lingmell down to Wasdale Head.

A third is by the footpath from the summit in the direction of Wastwater and Lingmell, bear right and pass to the right of Lingmell and follow the Guides Route above the top of Piers Ghyll.

If returning this way, on no account should an attempt be made to descend by the Piers Ghyll track, either drop after crossing Greta Ghyll or continue to the top of Sty Head Pass.

The last variation, the roughest and most interesting, is to take the same path from the cairn as mentioned in the last two routes, but bear left at the fork 80 yards from the summit. Soon the track is passing big boulders which require great care, then it drops to that narrow ridge separating Scafell Pike and Scafell known as Mickledore. Keep right, cross the ridge to the rock face of Scafell, turn right, keeping close to the side of the rocks, and follow the path down some steep and very rough scree to the bottom of Lord's Rake, the long scree shoot which rises between two buttresses. That is the route up Scafell (see Route 104), but for Wasdale, turn right with your back towards the crags and continue down some rough loose scree for about a hundred yards when the ground becomes firmer and more grassy. Make for the top of the rise in front, keeping to the right of the beck, and so to the top of Brown Tongue which you descend to Wasdale as described above. *The circular distance is 7 to 8 miles according to the route chosen. Time, 2½ to 3½ hours for the climb, rather less for the return.*

Route 109. SCAFELL. This is not an easy fell to climb from Wasdale Head. For the stranger the practical route is to follow the Burnmoor Track from Wasdale Head towards Eskdale as far as Burnmoor Tarn, then turn left and climb by the left of Hardrigg Ghyll, which flows into the tarn. The corner can be cut off by starting to climb where the track from Wasdale comes on to the open fell. Keep climbing towards the left of the summit, there is a path higher up, then this suddenly swings right up rocky ground to the summit.

It is a long tedious climb this way and the route is better used for the descent.

Another route which requires a certain amount of care is to climb by the Brown Tongue Route. This leaves the Wasdale Head road near the old school, and is signposted across two fields, crosses the river by a footbridge, then over a stile to the right, and the path is easy to follow round the side of Lingmell to the stream at the foot of Brown Tongue. Leave the path and climb up the fell side on the right, keeping to the right of the crags, then, when clear of these, bear left over the top to the summit.

The other choice, which is rough and requires great care, is by Lord's Rake, and the inexperienced mountaineer is well advised to leave this alone unless with some more experienced leader. The route is to the top of Brown Tongue then on towards Mickledore. At the foot of the scree, bear right towards the foot of the crags about fifty yards below Mickledore, to the foot of Lord's Rake, then follow as described in Route 104.

Route 110. GREAT GABLE. The best ascent is to the top of Sty Head Pass, then turn left at the signpost and follow the well-marked path to the summit (see Route 26).

The return can be made in the same way, but for a more interesting alternative, follow the path which starts in a line from the War Memorial on the cairn. This swings right, descends some very rough rocky ground, then swings left to the depression known as Windy Gap, separating Great Gable and Green Gable. A footpath starts on the left (avoid the one that drops towards Ennerdale), and keeps well in to the side of the fell, below the fine rock face of Gable on the Ennerdale side. Once clear of the crags the path drops towards the depression between Gable and Kirk Fell, then joined by a path from Brandreth, which is Moses Sledgate, an old smugglers' route. Between Wasdale and Buttermere, it swings left, keeping to the left of the beck which flows between here and Kirk Fell, and next drops down a long grassy tongue known as Gavel Neese, joining Sty Head Pass at the bottom near to Wasdale Head. Gavel Neese is rather a hard climb to do in the reverse direction. *7 miles. Ascent takes 2 to 2½ hours, descent by smugglers' route 2 hours.*

ENNERDALE

ENNERDALE IS ANOTHER NEGLECTED Lakeland valley; the lake, formerly called Broadwater, is two and a half miles long and three-quarters of a mile wide. At the head of the lake stretches the Liza Valley, over five miles in length, down which flows the River Liza from its source on the side of Great Gable, whose northern crags face down the valley. To the right of Gable is Kirk Fell, then across Looking Stead to Pillar with its famous Pillar Rock, until 1826 considered to be inaccessible, but since a favourite with rock climbers. It is best viewed from the valley immediately below the Rock, or it can be approached from the top of Pillar Mountain.

The nearest regular bus service is Rowrah, three miles, and Wath Brow, three and a half miles away. There is a good road from either place to Ennerdale Bridge, the village that lies a mile to the west of the lake, and the usual approach. Another route from Rowrah or Lamplugh by Croasdale misses the village on its way to the lake.

From the village a good road leads towards Croasdale, and just under a mile a road branches off to the right to How Hall, a farmhouse which was formerly a mansion of some note; a cross on the gable end of the barn and a pointed window or two on the far side indicate its antiquity. Passing through a gateway, the road descends sharply to reach the lake.

There is another route to the lake from Ennerdale Bridge, starting in the same direction but forking to the right half a mile from the bridge. Take the next road to the left, then to the right, to cross the river just before reaching the waterworks building. A cart track from here passes through two fields and reaches the lake by the waterhouse and weir where the River Ehen leaves the lake.

AROUND ENNERDALE

Route 111. ROUND DENT. Proceed by road to Wath Bridge. A fell road starts some fifty yards to the Ennerdale side of the bridge and rises sharply up a steep incline. At the top the route levels out and continues for about half-a-mile to a gate. Pass through the gateway and continue along the valley until you join another, less than a mile beyond. Cross the beck and proceed down the side of it. Later it becomes a road: cross the bridge and continue through a plantation then down a lane: fork left at next junction past a farm and continue along the road to Egremont.

The main point of interest in Egremont is the old castle which stands on a fell overlooking the town, and the grounds are laid out in pleasant gardens. The bus stop is in the main street opposite the War Memorial.

Return in the Cleator bus to Wath Brow, then walk to Ennerdale Bridge. *Wath Brow to Egremont by Ulldale, 5 miles.*

Route 112. DENT. Dent is a small conical-shaped fell 1,130 feet high. It can be climbed within the hour and the view from the summit is very extensive.

H

By road to Wath Bridge. Start along the road from the bridge on the left side of the river. About a mile along is a farm on the right, and just beyond a track starts through a gateway on the left and winds up the fell side, joining another track from Dent Farm, which lies on the side of the fell to the right. Turn left along here through a wood, until a fence coming directly from the top of the hill is reached. Follow this to the summit.

An easier approach from Wath Brow, although slightly longer, is to follow Route 111 as far as the gate which leads on to open fell. Do not pass through this gate, but through another, on your right, by the road which goes up through the forest; keep right at the first junction shortly after, where the road swings to the left. If you desire a more interesting walk, keep right up a footpath by the side of a disused road: at the top, turn left, and soon the track becomes a road again, crossing a beck by a large water tank. A pleasant half-mile walk, with occasional views between the trees, leads to the junction of the road you left near the bottom. There are two large water tanks just beyond, and from them a track goes up the hill on your right to the summit of Dent ('Long Barrow' on some maps). There is an extensive view from the top (marked by weed-ridden pools) over West Cumbria and the Solway. The actual summit of Dent is at a cairn about half-a-mile beyond.

Return to the water tanks. A few yards along the road to the right, a track starts on the left which goes down the side of a plantation to the river below at a bridge.

For Wath Brow go upstream for some half mile, then turn left into another valley and follow a footpath up the hillside to the left over Flat Fell; join a rough road on the far side leading to the gate at the end of the tarmac road for Wath Brow. For Egremont follow Route 111. You can also walk through the plantation of Lowther Park by the forest road which leads on to the main Ennerdale–Calderbridge road.

Route 113. CRAG FELL. From Ennerdale Bridge, start up the hill in the direction of Wath Brow and turn left at the top along the road signposted to Calder Bridge. The road rises gradually for about one and half miles, passes through a gate, then on the left will be observed a stone circle. The road next drops for a few yards, turns sharp left and begins to rise. About twenty yards beyond the turn a fell road starts on the left signposted "Red Beck". After the first half-mile, it enters and passes through a new plantation. At the first gate, a wire fence runs up the steep side of the fell. By climbing to the right of this fence the summit of Grike is reached in a few minutes and offers a good view of Ennerdale.

Continuing along the Pennington Mines road, the top of Crag Fell appears in sight in front, a little to the left. When in a direct line

between Crag Fell summit and Windscale leave the road and strike
across the fell side to the top of Crag Fell. There is a magnificent view
of Pillar Mountain and the Liza Valley, and almost the whole of
Ennerdale Lake with Great Borne behind and Red Pike and High Side
Stile to the right.

Start from the top with the lake on your right, but beware of the
high crags on the lake side of the fell. Do not start dropping until a
wire fence is reached, then descend to the right of it. The incline
is very steep at first but a short way down it becomes much easier,
and soon a good footpath appears which crosses a beck and cuts
diagonally down the side of Grike to Crag Farm in the bottom.
Cross a stone stile and follow the road from the farm over the river
back to Ennerdale Bridge. *10 miles. (Moderate.)*

Route 114. AROUND ENNERDALE LAKE. This walk is an ideal
outing for those desiring a pleasant walk lasting three to four hours.
It requires little direction as there is a good track all the way round
the lake. On one side is the road by the foot of Bowness Knott,
and on the other a pleasant footpath along the fell bottom. The
only time the track leaves the lake side is at the head of the lake where
it crosses the river by a footbridge half a mile beyond. *6 miles. (Easy.)*

Route 115. CALDER ABBEY. By Whitehaven bus to Wath
Brow, Cleator bus to Egremont, Seascale bus to Calder Bridge.

Leave the main road at the Calder Bridge bus stop by the secondary
road to the left of the church. A mile up this road, on the right,
stands the beautifully situated ruins of Calder Abbey. The abbey was
founded in 1134 and occupied by a band of monks from Furness
Abbey. Five years later it was attacked by the Scots and the monks
returned to their mother abbey. Later another colony came to
Calder and remained until the Dissolution.

Leaving the abbey, the road crosses the River Calder by Stakes
Bridge and continues up the valley for a further one and a half miles
to Thornholme, near the junction of the Rivers Calder and Wormgill,
an oasis in a desolate country, for while the land higher up is bare
fell land, this portion is beautifully wooded.

From Thornholme, cross the Wormgill and walk up the left side
passing some ancient British Settlement remains. Near the top of the
valley, cross over Stockdale Moor to the River Bleng and descend the
left side to a plantation. Follow a road through this until you cross the
river near a farm, and continue down the road to Gosforth.

Or from Thornholme, you continue by crossing the Wormgill by a
footbridge, follow a path up the right side of the Calder (the left-hand
river) for a mile to Matty Benn's Bridge, an old pack-horse bridge in
a beautiful setting, which probably dates back to the Normans.
Cross the bridge and proceed through the fields to pass the nearest

farm, and shortly after a road is reached which can be followed back to Ennerdale Bridge. *10 miles. (Easy.)*

To return to Egremont or Calderbridge, after crossing Matty Bann's Bridge, turn left through the field to the nearest gate from where a rough farm road goes uphill to the cross roads at Cold Fell Gate where there is a choice of roads to Calderbridge, Haile, Egremont or Ennerdale.

Route 116. RED PIKE. This is an interesting ridge walk that should not be missed. Starting from Ennerdale Bridge, follow the Croasdale road as far as the third junction to the right and turn up the latter, which goes up a hill to a farm and continues by a very narrow road until it joins another road from Croasdale near to a farm. Opposite the farm start up a lane towards the fell. Passing through two gateways, this becomes a mere footpath. Opposite the sharp end of Herdus, leave the path, cross the beck and a fence and climb up the End. From the bottom it appears steep and rough, but is much easier than it seems and forty minutes' steady climbing should take the average walker to the top.

A footpath continues along the fell side, the summit of Great Borne on the left can be included if desired, and passes to the right of Starling Dodd's summit towards Red Pike. The gradient is very easy until the final short, sharp rise to the summit of Red Pike, which has been in view in front all the way from Herdus End.

Continuing the walk in the same direction, the next summit, High Stile, is reached in a few minutes, and although higher than Red Pike the view is not so good. The path continues along the ridge towards High Crag. Take care to avoid the crags on the left of the ridge; on the right is some steep scree. Buttermere lies below on the left and Great Gable is prominent in front.

From the top of High Crag, descend in the direction of Haystacks and keep to the right on to Scarth Gap Pass. Shortly after leaving the summit to drop towards Ennerdale, a footpath starts to the right which falls diagonally down the side of High Crag to join the Liza Valley road about a mile below the foot of Scarth Gap. Follow the road down the valley by the lake to Ennerdale Bridge. *17½ miles. (Strenuous.)* This walk can be shortened by about six miles by descending direct to Gillerthwaite from Red Pike.

Route 117. PILLAR. Take the road by the lake as far as Gillerthwaite. Proceed about a mile up the valley beyond the farms until the river can be crossed by a footbridge. Follow the banks of the river up the valley until clear of the plantation and follow the footpath from here up Steeple. Scoat Fell is the height to the right of the gap in the fells called Wind Gap. It is possible to miss Steeple, but it is worth climbing for the view, especially of the fine crags on the side of Pillar. Next cross Wind Gap on to Pillar. (See Route 107.)

The best way to return to Ennerdale is to take the path which ▨▨ starts from the bottom of Wind Gap and falls towards the Liza Valley, then down beside the river along the same route as on the outward journey. An alternative is by the High Level Route which goes along the top of the plantation and then drops to Deep Gill. Cross bridges over Deep Gill and Silvercove Beck and follow footpath through woods down to Gillerthwaite Bridge over the Liza. *16 miles. (Strenuous.)*

Route 118. GREAT GABLE. To climb this fell from Ennerdale entails a long walk up the Liza Valley to the foot of Scarth Gap Pass. Next continue up the tongue between Great Gable and Brandreth on to Windy Gap. Turn right and follow the footpath to the summit of Great Gable. (See Route 26.)

Return by the same route to Windy Gap, then if a different return route is desired, follow the path from the Gap towards Ennerdale, but keeping well up to the left beneath the crags of the north face of Gable. After passing the crags, the path begins to drop towards a depression and on the far side will be observed a footpath leading up Kirk Fell in front. Follow this path to the summit and descend the other side in the direction of Scarth Gap Pass which can be seen across the valley. This path joins the Black Sail Pass near the bottom and the road down the valley is now followed back to Ennerdale. *Distance from Gillerthwaite and back, 13 miles. (Strenuous.)*

FOREST TRAILS

A new Forest Trail starts on the left of the Gillerthwaite road, about half a mile from Bowness Green Car Park, and is signposted.

Follow the yellow waymarks and you can enjoy a pleasant walk through the plantation, with a viewpoint and some seats near a new bridge over Smithy Beck.

Continue past the second seat to the next marker where you join a forest road which leads down to the lake at Smithy Beck Bridge. This is half the walk. To do the full round from the waterfall join the road and proceed up the hill, through the gate to the remains of some old Settlements on the right. Shortly after, the waymarked route rises to the right and continues through the plantation, finally descending to the lake.

A descriptive map/guide to this, and the longer 'Nine Becks Walk' can be purchased from a box beside the gate over the road near the car park at Bowness Green. The circular walk from Bowness Car Park is just over four miles. The 'Nine Becks Walk' is waymarked by blue circles and is nine miles long

THE BUTTERMERE VALLEY

THE BUTTERMERE VALLEY is the only Cumberland valley to possess three lakes—Buttermere, Crummock Water and Loweswater.

Buttermere is a charming lake, one and a quarter miles long, half a mile wide, set deep in a basin of fells which descend almost sheer into the lake on two sides, well wooded with Scotch fir and larch. The lake is famous for its reflections and is a great favourite with artists and photographers.

Scale Force

Crummock Water is the largest of the three, being three and a half miles long and three-quarters of a mile wide. Its most imposing features are Melbreak, the fell to the west, and Rannerdale Knott, a small headland jutting out into the lake opposite Melbreak. The main road runs round the end of Rannerdale Knott and there is a good footpath below Melbreak. About a mile up Scale Beck, which flows into the lake to the south of Melbreak, is Scale Force, the highest waterfall in England, having a drop of 120 feet. It is set deep in a big ravine abounding with copse and fern, but is not as attractive as many other Lakeland falls.

Loweswater

Loweswater lies about one hundred feet higher than Crummock, into which lake it flows by a small river, and is of similar size to Buttermere. Its shores are well wooded; the road runs along one side and a cart-track through Holme Woods on the other.

Fairy Dell

Buttermere village is in a charming situation at the foot of Buttermere Hause, between the two lakes of Buttermere and Crummock. There are several pleasant easy strolls in the neighbourhood. One is opposite the Bridge Inn up Fairy Dell, others are to the left of the Fish Hotel to the shores of Buttermere, or to the right after the hotel to the shores of Crummock. There is also a pleasant stroll to Crummock through Long How Wood which starts a short distance along the Cockermouth road after leaving the Bridge Inn.

English Stronghold

Buttermere has an interesting history dating back to the time of the Norman Conquest, for it was in this valley that the English made their secret headquarters for attacks upon the Norman invaders. Although the Normans eventually attacked with an overwhelmingly large army, they suffered a heavy defeat and Buttermere remained the only valley that they did not succeed in capturing.

The River Cocker flows from Crummock down the Vale of Lorton
to Cockermouth. The village of Lorton lies midway down the valley
at the foot of Whinlatter Pass; it is divided into two, High and Low,
with the village church midway between. High Lorton is
exceptionally picturesque.

COCKERMOUTH

At Cockermouth, the river empties into the River Derwent which
in turn flows into the Solway Firth at Workington. Cockermouth is
an interesting market town (market day, Monday), and is an
excellent centre for exploring Cumbria by bus. Buses radiate in all
directions to Keswick, Carlisle, Workington, Maryport (for Allonby
and Silloth), Blindcrake, Whitehaven, Lamplugh, Ennerdale,
Loweswater and Buttermere. It is well equipped with hotels and
provides a convenient centre for a holiday.

Wordsworth Birthplace
There is a public park containing tennis courts, bowling greens and
amusements for children. Another attraction is the castle which
stands near the entrance to the town from the Keswick direction. It
was built from the square-hewn stones of the Roman 'Oppidum'
and was the scene of a big battle with the Royalists in 1648. It has
some unique dungeons and a wonderful view of the surrounding
country from the terrace walk. The castle is open to visitors on certain
days. Cockermouth is the birthplace of the famous Lakeland poet,
William Wordsworth, whose parents came to reside here in 1766. The
house, open to the public, stands in the main street and is National
Trust property. At the village of Eaglesfield nearby was born Robert de
Eaglesfield, who founded the Queen's College, Oxford, in 1340; and
also John Dalton, the chemist, in 1766.

AROUND THE BUTTERMERE VALLEY

Where the starting point is reached by bus in the Vale of Lorton,
take the Cockermouth bus from Buttermere, or the Buttermere bus
from Cockermouth. The bus terminus at Buttermere is the Bridge
Hotel, and in Cockermouth the main street.

Route 119. LOW FELL. By bus to Low Lorton. Cross the river
by the road bridge in Low Lorton and go along the road to the
left for one and a quarter miles to the cottages at Thrackthwaite.
Immediately past the last house on the right turn up a lane on the
same side towards Smithy Fell, turn right at the top along a pony-

track which soon begins to rise sharply by a series of zigzag bends to the summit of the route, where an iron gate is reached. Turn left along the side of the fence as far as Watching Crag, about fifty yards distance from where is one of the finest views of Crummock and the upper Vale of Lorton.

Return to the path, proceed down the other side, cross the depression on your right, round the end of the next rise, and then down to a gateway to join the Mosser Fell road farther down. Turn left along here to join the Loweswater road, and follow it to Crummock. The road descends to the valley, crosses the river and climbs sharply to Scale Hill Hotel. Half a mile farther on, at a road fork, the Cockermouth—Buttermere bus can be caught. The bus also runs alongside Loweswater.

A good plan if returning to Buttermere is to leave the road at the foot of Scale Hill immediately after crossing the river and turn through a gate on the right. A wide track goes through the wood; keep right at the first fork and left at the second, then the path goes close to the lake, about twenty feet above it to the boat landing. Continue along the path by the lake side to Cinderdale Common and either walk or bus to Buttermere. *8 miles. (Moderate.)*

Route 120. AROUND BUTTERMERE. There is a good footpath almost the whole of the way round the shores of Lake Buttermere; the only place it leaves the lake shore is at the lake head where it makes a slight diversion round by Gategarth Farm.

Starting to the left of the Fish Hotel, the track is easy to follow and requires no further explanation. It is interesting to note that in one part the path has been tunnelled through the rock opposite Hassness. *5 miles. (Easy.)*

Route 121. AROUND CRUMMOCK AND LOWESWATER. By Keswick or Cockermouth bus to Cinderdale Common. Cross ladder stile over the stone wall, and follow footpath above the lake shore, this leads to Lanthwaite Woods, continue through the woods, keeping left at junctions until it joins the main road at Scale Hill Bridge.

For Loweswater, proceed along the main road from Scale Hill, passing the interesting church at Kirk Stile to its right, and soon Loweswater is reached. The road goes along its entire length. Opposite The Grange Hotel, which is the last building on the right before the road rises sharply up Fangs Brow, a cart-track starts and goes up a lane to Hudson Place Farm. Turn left at the farm along the track ,which drops to the lake, and goes through the pretty Holme Woods by the lake shore. Holme Force is an attractive small waterfall a short distance up the only beck which is crossed in the wood.

At the first farm, Watergate, at the end of the lake, the track turns left through two fields and joins a road coming from High Nook, beside High Nook Beck. Turn left and soon the main road is joined. Turn right along here as far as Kirk Stile, turn right to pass between the church and inn, and follow the road to Highpark. A footpath starts from here which follows the lake shore below Melbreak; it is wet in places. Upon reaching Scale Beck, which flows down to the lake a short distance beyond the end of Melbreak, it is worth the extra mile diversion to visit Scale Force, England's highest waterfall which lies higher up the beck.

Passing beyond the head of the lake the track goes by the river for a short distance until it can be crossed by a bridge, then, crossing some fields, it finishes at Buttermere village. *Distance, around Crummock, 9 miles, two lakes, 15 miles. (Easy.)*

Route 122. MELBREAK. Melbreak is a moderate and interesting climb within easy distance of Buttermere. From the village, start down the left of the Fish Hotel and follow the track over the river and by the shores of Crummock as far as Scale Beck. Proceed a short distance up the beck along the footpath, then, when opposite the end of Melbreak, the fell on your immediate right, leave the track and climb up the end of Melbreak. Walk along the table-like top to descend the far end slightly to the left, opposite Bargate. The descent entails some scrambling down rough scree between the crags and requires care, but this can be avoided if desired by descending to the left into Mosedale a short distance before reaching the north-western end of Melbreak. Join the road leading to Kirk Stile, turn right down the hill and cross the river. Turn right through the gate at the foot of the hill and follow the track through the woods.

If returning to Buttermere on foot, keep right so as to follow the lake shore as far as possible, until the path joins the road near Cinderdale. To return by bus, keep left until the track reaches the main road at Lanthwaite Green. *Distance right round, 10 miles. (Moderate.)*

Route 123. SAIL BECK, KESWICK. The normal way to do this walk is to follow the main road over Buttermere Hause and Newlands to Portinscale, but a more interesting route for the walker is to start up Buttermere Hause, by the church, and a short distance along the road drop to the left and cross the river to join a track on the far side. Or this track can be joined at its start through the wooded dell, opposite the Bridge Hotel, or from behind the post office up the road.

The track runs by the Sail Beck at an easy gradient at first, then rises fairly sharply between Sail and Ard Crags, dropping down the other side of the rise by Rigg Beck, joining the Newlands Road at the bottom. Continue along the main road and keep left at the first fork to Braithwaite. A short cut starts at the wood on the left of the road (after passing some scree) by a grassy track, past Braithwaite Lodge to join the road near the inn. *Buttermere to Braithwaite, 8 miles. (Moderate.)*

To reach Keswick on foot, from Rigg Beck, proceed down the road and take the first fork right to Stair. Cross the river and proceed up a narrow road immediately opposite to Skelghyll, pass by the farm bearing left to a gate at the top of the hill, then along the road to a cattle grid. Just below, a path starts on the right, dropping to another narrow road, almost immediately across this road, another lane (signposted 'Portinscale') starts, leading to the entrance of Lingholme.

Cross this road and follow a path through the wood which joins a road near to Derwent Bank Holiday Fellowship Centre. Continue to the Derwentwater Hotel, turn right beyond, cross the River Derwent, and then by a footpath to the right which leads to Keswick. *Three miles from Braithwaite to Keswick.*

Route 124. RED PIKE, HIGH STILE. From Buttermere village, start to the left of the Fish Hotel, and follow the track to the foot of Buttermere, crossing the river by a wooden footbridge. Almost immediately opposite, to the left of Sour Milk Ghyll, a footpath starts and rises through the plantation, emerging at the top on to open fell. It swings round in a semi-circle to cross the beck near to Bleaberry Tarn. The tarn lies in a huge saucer, and the path goes round the saucer edge on the right up to the summit of Red Pike. Follow Route 116 to High Crag, and drop down to the left on to the top of Scarth Gap Pass. Turn left down the pass and left again at the bottom to return along the shores of Buttermere to the village. *7 miles. (Strenuous.)*

Route 125. HAYSTACKS. By road to Buttermere. Follow the previous route to the footbridge at the outlet of Buttermere, cross the bridge and continue by the path along the shore to the head of the lake. Take the track which branches to the right and joins the path from Gatesgarth to the top of Scarth Gap Pass.

From the summit of the pass, marked by a cairn, turn left and make your way by the path up between the crags to the summit cairn which can be seen on the top of Haystacks.

Haystacks consists of a rather large top on which are several small peaks, all marked by O.S. cairns. Between several are some mountain pools, the largest of which is Innominate Tarn. The view includes Buttermere, Crummock and Ennerdale lakes, and a very fine fell aspect which includes the Pillar, Great Gable, Fleetwith Pike and Robinson.

The path goes to the left of Innominate Tarn, crosses a very deep gully, which should not be used to return to Buttermere, then winds round to the right below more crags, and crosses the beck close to the foot of Black Beck Tarn. It next passes to the right of two small fells, winding left round the far side of the second and drops to cross the beck and join the pony-track on the far side coming down from the disused quarries. Continue down the track into Warnscale Bottom and on to Gatesgarth, return by the lake shore to Buttermere village. This walk is equally attractive in the opposite direction. *9 miles. (Moderate.)*

Route 126. GRASMOOR. By Cockermouth or Keswick bus to Lanthwaite Green. From Lanthwaite Green Farm, cross the Green opposite the farm and over Gaskill Ghyll by a footbridge. A path starts and begins to rise round the end of Whiteside and continues up the deep ghyll by a good footpath to almost the top of the rise. The beck turns sharp right and the footpath does likewise, following the beck for a short distance before crossing it and continuing to the top of Grasmoor.

Grasmoor is fairly flat on the top and the best view is obtained by walking a short distance west towards Crummock. The three lakes are seen below, and behind the fells is an extensive view over West Cumbria to the Solway Firth. Close at hand on the left is Robinson, separated from Grasmoor by the wide valley of Buttermere Hause. Begin to descend in this direction until a narrow ridge is reached, turn right and follow this ridge down Wandope, Whiteless Pike and Blake Rigg to Buttermere. *7 miles. (Fairly strenuous.)*

Route 127. ROBINSON. Start up Buttermere Hause by the church, about one hundred yards along a path starts on the right and winds up the fell side to the top of Buttermere Moss. Crossing a piece of level boggy ground, it begins to rise again at the far end, bearing left to the summit of Robinson, a fine viewpoint. Loweswater and Crummock can be seen and, by walking a few yards north, Derwentwater comes into view. Scafell Pike summit is directly behind the summit of Great Gable.

Drop down the grassy slope towards Dale Head and follow the wire fence on to the top of Dale Head. Descend to the left of a wire fence by a good path to the slate works at the top of Honister Pass.

Turn right down the pass and follow the road to Gatesgarth, and to Buttermere by the lake shore. *10 miles. (Strenuous.)*

Route 128. GREAT GABLE. By the lake shore to Gatesgarth. Pass through the gate beyond the farm at Gatesgarth, turn right along a track round the foot of Fleetwith Pike, by Warnscale Bottom, which rises on the left of the beck, crossing it about half a mile up. The footpath now strikes diagonally across the side of Brandreth until it reaches the summit of a long ridge. Thence as Route 26 to the top of Great Gable.

To descend, start out in the direction of Kirk Fall, and drop to the left of the crags on the north face of Gable to join the footpath between Gable and Kirk Fell. The path goes north-east below Gillercombe Head, then north-west towards Haystacks. Cross over Haystacks and descend to Scarth Gap, following this down to the lake; keep left, and follow the lake side footpath through the woods to cross the footbridge at the foot of the lake and then back to Buttermere village. *14 miles. (Strenuous.)*

MOUNTAINS ABOVE 2,000 FEET

	Feet		Feet
SCAFELL PIKE	3,206	CARRS	2,575
SCAFELL	3,162	GLARAMARA	2,560
HELVELLYN	3,118	KIDSTY PIKE	2,560
SKIDDAW	3,053	RED SCREES	2,541
GREAT END	2,984	WANDOPE	2,533
BOWFELL	2,960	CAUDALE MOOR	2,502
GREAT GABLE	2,949	WETHERLAM	2,502
PILLAR	2,927	HIGH RAISE	2,500
ESK PIKE	2,903	RED PIKE (Buttermere)	2,479
FAIRFIELD	2,863	ILL BELL	2,476
SADDLEBACK	2,847	DALE HEAD	2,473
CRINKLE CRAGS	2,816	HIGH CRAG	2,443
DOLLYWAGGON PIKE	2,810	ROBINSON	2,417
GRASMOOR	2,791	SEAT SANDAL	2,415
ST. SUNDAY CRAG	2,751	HARRISON STICKLE	2,403
EEL CRAG	2,749	HINDSCARTH	2,385
LITTLE SCOAT FELL	2,746	ULLSCARF	2,370
HIGH STREET	2,718	FROSWICK	2,359
STEEPLE	2,687	PIKE O'STICKLE	2,323
LINGMELL	2,649	PIKE O'BLISCO	2,304
HIGH STILE	2,643	SEATALLAN	2,266
CONISTON OLD MAN	2,633	PLACE FELL	2,154
KIRKFELL	2,631	HARTER FELL (Eskdale)	2,140
SWIRL HOW	2,630	FLEETWITH PIKE	2,126
RED PIKE (Wasdale)	2,629	HONISTER CRAG	2,070
HAYCOCK	2,619	YEWBARROW	2,058
GRISEDALE PIKE	2,593	GREAT BORNE	2,019
HARTER FELL (Mardale)	2,585	CAUSEY PIKE	2,000

HEIGHTS AND LOCATIONS OF WATERFALLS

	Feet	
SCALE FORCE	125	1 mile S.W. of Crummock Water.
BARROW FALLS ..	108	Behind Barrow House, Derwentwater.
LODORE FALLS.. ..	90	Behind Lodore Hotel, Derwentwater.
AIRA FORCE	70	Half-mile west of Ullswater.
STOCKGILL FORCE ..	60	¾-mile east of Ambleside.
DALEGARTH FORCE ..	60	1¼ miles south of Boot, Eskdale.
LOW BIRKER FORCE ..	60	1 mile S.E. of Boot, Eskdale.
DUNGEON GHYLL FORCE	60	Behind New Dungeon Ghyll Hotel, Langdale.
DASH FALLS	60	Between Skiddaw and Overwater.
RYDAL UPPER FALLS ..	60	East of Rydal.
COLWITH FORCE ..	45	Near Colwith Bridge.

HEIGHTS AND LOCATIONS OF PASSES

	Feet	
ESK HAUSE	2,490	Sty Head Tarn—Angle Tarn.
STICKS	2,420	Thirlmere—Ullswater.
NAN BIELD ..	2,100	Haweswater—Kentmere.
COLEDALE ..	2,000	Crummock—Braithwaite.
ROSSETT GHYLL ..	2,000	Angle Tarn—Dungeon Ghyll.
GREENUP EDGE ..	1,995	Stonethwaite—Grasmere.
WALNA SCAR ..	1,990	Coniston—Duddon.
GATESGARTH ..	1,950	Haweswater—Kendal.
GRISEDALE ..	1,929	Grasmere—Patterdale.
BLACK SAIL ..	1,800	Ennerdale (head)—Wasdale Head.
SCANDALE ..	1,750	Ambleside—Brotherswater.
STY HEAD ..	1,600	Seathwaite—Wasdale Head.
STAKE	1,576	Dungeon Ghyll—Langstrath.
KIRKSTONE ..	1,576	Ambleside—Brotherswater.
GARBURN ..	1,450	Windermere—Kentmere.
SCARF GAP ..	1,400	Buttermere—Ennerdale (head).
FLOUTERN TARN ..	1,300	Crummock—Ennerdale Lake.
HARD KNOTT ..	1,290	Eskdale—Cockley Beck.
WRYNOSE ..	1,270	Cockley Beck—Little Langdale.
HONISTER ..	1,190	Buttermere—Seatoller.
NEWLANDS (Buttermere Hause)	1,096	Buttermere—Portinscale.
WHINLATTER ..	1,043	Lorton—Braithwaite.
DUNMAIL RAISE ..	782	Thirlmere—Grasmere.

Index